Trust Me

The Untold Story of Mary Magdalene
A Novel Story

Anne Urne

FIRST EDITION

BOIS PUBLICATIONS
OKLAHOMA CITY, OKLAHOMA

BOIS PUBLICATIONS
OKLAHOMA CITY, OKLAHOMA

Cover Design: Susan Brubeck McCubbin
                       Media3 / www.media3.cc

Cover Photographer: Susan Brubeck McCubbin

Printed in the United States of America by Media3, Sausalito, CA

First Printing: May 2004
Second Printing: March 2011
10 9 8 7 6 5 4 3 2

Published by
BOIS Publications
5411 Colfax Place
Oklahoma City, OK 73112

ISBN 0-9727967-1-1

Library of Congress Cataloging-in-Publication Data

Urne, Anne
  Trust ME

Library of Congress Control Number: 2004100215

ALSO BY ANNE URNE:

A SPIRITUAL TRILOGY

- Way Beyond The River
- The Walls Came Tumbling Down
- It Came to Pass

For Casey: This is the one . . .

ACKNOWLEDGEMENT

Heartfelt thanks go out to Susan Brubeck McCubbin. I am so proud to have Susan partnering with me to bring this book to life. With her business savvy she brings sparkling energy, brilliant ideas and business acumen to handle the advertising, marketing and web development for this book. Susan created the jacket design and is also providing printing services through her company, Media3 in Sausalito.

Timing is everything and now is the time for this book to be mass marketed. The book has been waiting since its initial printing in 2004 for this moment in time. I lost my mother this year, and out of that loss came a reconnection with my remarkable cousin, Susan Brubeck McCubbin, that was decades overdue. After so many years the family connection and childhood memories are as fond and vibrant as ever. So, too, is this book alive and ready to be shared and enjoyed.

TRUST ME

The Untold Story of Mary Magdalene

PROLOGUE

Oh my, look at the time. I'll have to start getting ready for work in thirty minutes! I need to talk to my daughter.

Anne was anxious to read her the letter she had composed for a prospective publisher.

I was actually trembling with excitement over breakfast, she recalled as she sat down on her bed next to the phone.

She always calls around 7:30, and it's 7 now. I'll just try to rest a few minutes before getting ready for work and wait for her call.

She leaned back against the pillows and started to read the letter again. Rrring!

"Hey, Michelle, I was wanting you to call!"

"I know. That's why I called now."

"You are always in tune to me, my darling child. You must have felt my excitement!"

"Yes, I did. So, what's going on with you this morning?"

Michelle faithfully called her Mom every morning to chat, after running with her dogs around the lake, fixing her son's breakfast, seeing her husband off and then getting herself ready for work. Her high energy and enthusiasm erupted through the phone lines each morning teasing her mother because she always sounded confused when she answered the cordless phone. It just didn't work like the regular phone, and all Michelle ever heard when her mother answered was the last syllable of hel – 'lo'.

Teasingly she would echo back to her, "hello, hello" and her mother would always laugh and say, "is anybody in there?"

Michelle was the apple of her Mom's eye. She was so proud of her. Michelle was her beautiful strawberry blonde with flashing green eyes. She still had her high school gymnast figure and the energy that went with it. It was hard to believe that her son was in high school. Anne still thought of herself as a young woman, though a baby boomer, she realized every day that her daughter was getting closer to 40 and she was getting farther and farther away.

"I've been up since 3:30 trying to do some more work on my book. I felt so badly about Casey's car engine burning up. It seemed to give me the inspiration I needed to get busy writing again. I promised him that when Grandma sold one of her books she would buy him whatever car he liked."

"Yes, he has been pretty down since his car broke. He has put so much work and money into rebuilding that old Super Sport, and I think he is about to decide he would rather have a normal car."

"Well, that's why I wanted to talk to you. Instead of adding another chapter to my book, this really great letter just manifested itself while I was writing. I mean, it is so good! It amazes me because it reads like something that was given to me - instead of created by me. You know what I mean?"

Of course, she knew. She was my confidante and she knew all my quirks and intimate thoughts.

Michelle listened while her Mom read the letter over the phone.

"You know what impresses me in your letter? It is the confidence that comes across. And, I know from experience, that once you have the confidence to do something, then you do succeed. It reminds me of my golf game. I have confidence in my long shot, and I always hit that one really well. I'm still working on perfecting my putt."

"I will start sending it out and see what happens. I still have to finish the book, but this one needs a publisher that can market it. Tell Casey that Grandma is still trying to get that book published for him. Guess I better get ready for work - hope I can stay awake all day! I love you."

"I love you, too! Have a great day, talk to you later."

Anne plugged in the curlers and started putting in her contacts. Her hair was prettier than it had been at age 40, because Michelle was the best colorist in the city and she weaved her red, gold and coppery highlights back into her hair every six weeks to camouflage any gray that might spring up.

She stood in front of the mirror and checked out the suit she had selected, the heels and her hair. Everything checked out and she was happy with her size 6 figure. Not bad for a girl in her early fifties!

She knew her husband appreciated her nice appearance, even if he did complain about the high cost of maintenance. Anne knew too, that even though Al was 20 years her senior, he was still a handsome man with an eye for an attractive girl and she planned to always be that girl. She loved to tease her husband and thanks to his great tolerance and patience she was able to get by with it. He would sometimes warn her though that she might need a "knot on her head" - but Anne knew he was only kidding. He was her strength and her happiness. She adored him. He looked 15 years younger than his age and possessed great charm, wit and intelligence. He was very special and Anne knew it.

Anne recalled her excitement over her new book. It had started out as a spiritual non-fiction, much a continuation of her previous books. But, all of a sudden it had taken an unexpected turn. She knew this one would have to be published as a fiction, and now she was faced with a very challenging task. She recalled the specific incident that had triggered the domino effect that would change her latest book from a quiet spiritual journey into an intriguing mystery novel. In her wildest dreams she could never have imagined writing fiction, much less one that would involve murder, kidnapping and who knows what else. The pieces were still falling and they were coming down in a hail storm of information.

"You ought to read *the DaVinci Code,*" Barbara told Anne on a recent visit to her home. Anne's former boss was aware of her passion for biblical mysteries.

"From what I've heard it is blasphemous, alleging that Mary Magdalene was married to Jesus and conceived his child! I don't think I would be interested in reading about that. Besides, I've been getting back

into the grind of working again, after spending two
months recovering from my last hectic job."

"How is your blood pressure, now?"

"It's getting better, but I sure don't want to get locked
into another full time job!"

"You do seem to be commitment phobic," Barbara
observed.

"I suppose that's possible. I do prefer temp work,
because it doesn't compromise my free spirit."

Anne could pinpoint the seemingly insignificant visit
with Barbara as the spark that ignited her desire to learn
more about the Magdalene and her purported marriage.
An inner passion and curiosity for religious and spiritual
understanding were stirred to new heights and set Anne on
a path of determined spiritual investigation. She was
immediately taken into a new dimension of mystery solving
and her book in progress soared into an unexpected new
direction!

CHAPTER ONE

Some have entertained angels unawares. Awareness lifted Anne straight up out of bed at three this morning. She was expecting something today and she just couldn't sleep. Ten days ago she had awakened from a dream recalling vividly the words: *she will be married on the nineteenth.* She had been counting down the days expecting something great to happen in ten days.

Reading her Bible that morning took her to a verse in Revelations where she read, . . . *the devil is about to cast some of you into prison that you may be tested for ten days.*

Ten days? My dream of a marriage occurs in ten days! Something is about to happen.

Anne had no idea what it could be, but she had great expectations. On the morning of the 19th Anne awoke wondering what this day would bring, and she was reminded of the significant turns in her life. She recalled a beautiful woman whose appearances in her life had impacted just as many changes. She seemed to just pop up out of nowhere and each time she appeared, a great change took place. Anne knew that she was in town today.

Anne had phoned her mother a few days ago to plan a long overdue brunch for the girls. Oh, how they enjoyed getting together several times a year. They were about five or six ladies ranging in age from thirties to seventies. Anne's sister, Marcia, used to attend, but she had died suddenly several years ago.

Maureen was the mother of that beautiful woman, Oleta, who now lived in Washington D. C. She was a former state representative and Anne had the privilege of meeting her when she reported for a temp job 18 years ago. Oleta was running for lieutenant governor and had requested some help from the temp agency where Anne had just put in her application. It was at this campaign that she met her mother, Maureen. They hit it off and have been friends ever since.

Anne met and made many new and wonderful friends during that campaign and they have gotten together often ever since. Anne was especially fond of Maureen and Oleta because they were Irish, like her family.

Maureen is a remarkably intelligent lady with so much energy. She turned eighty this year and loves to go dancing every weekend. She told Anne how she was teaching line dancing to the other ladies at their singles club. Anne was delighted when Maureen said she wanted to buy a copy of her last book to send to her daughter.

"Oh, Maureen, I have already mailed her a copy."

She had sent it to her with a notation that she was the angel on page 264. She didn't mention this to Maureen, but told her she was sure she must have gotten it by now.

"Hey, I'm getting another call - I'll call you back." Maureen clicked off.

Anne finished preparing dinner. A few minutes later, the phone rang again.

"It's Maureen! Guess what?" she exclaimed excitedly. "That was Oleta that just called. She is in town and didn't want to call unless she would have time to see me; but said she could see me Saturday, and she told me she received your book!"

"Well that was certainly a speedy response to your request, wasn't it? I'll talk to you tomorrow and we'll see where to go for brunch in a few weeks."

Saturday wasn't just any day. Saturday was the 19th. The day Anne had been anticipating and she thought it more than just a coincidence that Oleta would be in town that day.

It was 3 o'clock on Saturday morning and Anne was wide awake.

What a difference Oleta had made in her life - not just once, but three times!

And, here, I am expecting some great thing to happen today - and she lands here on the very same day. This is one of those significant coincidences.

Anne knew that awareness of a significant coincidence was the key to the manifestation of a spiritual event. Her first significant liberating experience had been facilitated by this beautiful blue eyed blonde while she was running for state office.

Dreamily she recalled that time in 1986, an election year.

That was my year of significant change.

It was summer and she had just gotten out of the most miserable relationship of six years. She had been through hell and at long last the monster she had married was out of her life for good.

He had left her broke, jobless, homeless and without a car, but none of that mattered. Anne was so happy to be free. She had rented a small condo and was about to take her first temporary assignment at the offices of Oleta for Lieutenant Governor.

What excitement awaited her inside the doors of a statewide campaign office! *This is heaven!* Anne loved her new job. The teamwork and camaraderie were exhilarating. She was in her late thirties and she was alive again. The day Oleta came into the office, Anne thought she was just a beautiful college girl sitting on the front desk of the office talking to some of the staff. To her surprise - she was the candidate! She was only two years younger than Anne, but Oleta looked twenty and she had to convince people she was old enough to run for this office. Her young good looks were among the many challenges she faced in this race, as well as a dozen contenders!

Serious would begin to describe her. What an ambitious and accomplished politician she was. Her tenure in the House of Representatives was marked with greatness and achievement.

Yes, Anne remembered that change in her life had occurred with the appearance of this beautiful angel. Some people didn't think of her as an angel, however, because she was driven and could throw a good old Irish fit if she thought things weren't going as planned, and especially if she saw someone slacking off in their duties. This gal was a worker and she noticed Anne right off because she was a dedicated and hard worker. They clicked and after the campaign, she trusted Anne to close up her office. Oleta finished a rugged series of runoffs in a narrow defeat and took a new position at a law firm. She launched Anne into her new career in the legal field when she took her along and trained her as her assistant.

Up until then Anne's career had been in civil service. From medical secretary to safety officer, she had spent fourteen years working for the government. Her career along with her earthly possessions had all disappeared during her hellish marriage to a bona fide sociopath. Anne had been brought down so low emotionally and stressed so severely during that period of her life that she suffered a near death experience from stroke symptoms.

Oh, how happy she was the day she stepped into the campaign office. She was free, her life had started over and her grandson was born that year! People would comment on her extreme energy and happiness.

Oh, if they only knew where I'd been, she'd think. *After being released from hell, who wouldn't be happy!*

This was the first eventful change marked by Oleta's appearance. Anne fast forwarded her thoughts to 1992. Oleta was now living and working in Washington D. C. and Anne had recently married the man of her dreams. He was twenty years her senior and a retired county commissioner.

She met him after working as a scheduler on a campaign in 1990 for a gubernatorial candidate. They dated almost two years and then married. It was a busy summer in late June of 1992 and she was embroiled in another campaign for a U. S. Senate candidate when they married. Al lived in the country and Anne lived in the city. She commuted on the weekends the first few months, and then in November at the end of the campaign, she moved to the small town about 80 miles south of the city.

She had spent the past two years traveling back and forth between their homes and had watched in awe as Al maneuvered massive farm equipment planting and harvesting wheat. How handsome he looked riding horseback through the pastures as he checked on his cattle. He had a very gentle horse for Anne so she could ride with him and enjoy the wonder of it all. Her friends in the city couldn't believe she was enjoying it so much. They knew her as the girl that liked to dance every night of the week!

Life with Al was wonderful. After moving to the small town she enjoyed riding up and down those old country roads and listening to his stories about the history and people of the area.

Then winter set in and Anne had a whiplash of the reality that she wasn't working. Her accustomed fast paced environment in a law office or a frenzied campaign was abruptly changed to this new aura of stillness! Winter had set in, the wheat was growing and now what was she going to do?

Anne decided she would read some books to pass the time. Her mother, the consummate bookworm, always chided her because she didn't read, but Anne had always been in too big of a hurry to sit still. There wasn't any hurry now, so she went in search of reading material. First she considered novels then made an abrupt decision to read the Bible. A favorite evangelist had once said to expect a blessing after reading the New Testament within 30 days - so that was her goal and that was where she began.

Again, she recalled the crescendo of excitement that welled within her while reading and expecting that blessing. She remembers the day she finished the last page of the New Testament. She was like a kid waiting for Christmas!

Three days later she got a call from Oleta in D. C. asking if she could come up there for a couple of weeks to organize her office!

Wow! D. C. That sure beat spending the winter with nothing much to do! Yes, that memory will always remain with me.

She took that Bible with her and never missed reading it each night before going to bed.

She flew home just in time for Valentine's Day. Al was happy to see her when she arrived at the airport. He took her to a wonderful Italian restaurant for dinner in the city and reserved a room for them to spend the night.

They returned home to the little town, where it wasn't long until Al was called to work on the big earthquake that had just hit Los Angeles.

Anne marveled that her husband was so multitalented. Besides raising cattle and wheat, and serving as county commissioner for ten years, he had previously worked many years as an insurance claims manager and adjuster.

Off they raced to California! Life was full of surprises and it was anything but dull. They spent six busy months in L. A. Al took Anne along on his property inspections and she became his helper, assisting him in the grueling late night paperwork.

She learned the computer program that adjusters were now using and they made a great team. He was the consummate adjuster and she was his devoted assistant.

They returned home looking forward to a respite from their hard work. It was great to be back for a much needed rest. Anne wondered what to expect next.

Wouldn't you know? That angel appeared again. She called to tell Anne that her friend, a Supreme Court justice - no less, needed an assistant and she had recommended her.

That would mean, of course, that if she was selected and decided to take the job, she would have to move back to the city! *Oh, no! Oh, yes!!!!*

She had done it again! Al was so impressed and proud when Anne took this new job that he sold the country home and moved her back to the city.

Yes, thanks to Oleta, Anne was returning home to her daughter and grandson, not to mention her manicurist and friends, her mother, sister, and niece and nephew with their children. Everyone Anne loved was there.

There were more surprises waiting there. The one that stands out was the new home they found.

Anne's daughter came to see it and remarked, "Mom, this is exactly like the house you lost."

She was right! It was a carbon copy of the house Anne had grieved over losing during her previous marriage. Anne's life was unbelievably great since finding Al and the momentous changes could be traced right back to that cold winter day when she began reading her Bible. She found it hard to believe how much her life had changed for the better since 1986. It was 1994 and her life had turned completely around. The things she had painfully lost were being restored perfectly.

It has been nearly ten years since she returned home and the wonders never cease. She thinks of it as a journey full of wonderful surprises. Anne began recording this journey and her journal turned into three books that she compiled and published in a volume entitled *A Spiritual Trilogy*. That was the book Maureen wanted to buy for Oleta.

For three years in succession Anne finished a book right at Christmas time and so she had given copies to intimate friends and family.

Maureen was the one who encouraged her to publish. Of course, Anne had no connections so she self-published - fifty to start and now what do you do? She sold some, gave some away and re-edited the text so it would be ready whenever something happened to get it marketed. She trusted God would figure that part out - she surely couldn't. That was the best part of her spiritual journey, learning to trust God.

The nineteenth came and went without incident. She didn't talk to Maureen or Oleta. Regardless, Anne still wondered about the words she heard in her dream, *she will be married on the nineteenth.*

She knew the words held some meaning, and she also knew that the meaning would be shown to her when the time was right. For now, she just tucked them away in her memory and was not disappointed because she understood that spiritual time was different from the worldly calendar.

CHAPTER TWO

Anne had spent many hours researching the scriptures and apocryphal works over the past decade. She had voraciously studied many literary works and soon found herself on a path that was leading to surprising spiritual truths.

The very information contained in her previous books was, in fact, a far stretch from traditional beliefs.

Much like the controversial DaVinci Code, Anne too had written new concepts about biblical patriarchs that could be considered controversial.

But my books never questioned the divinity of Jesus!

She defended her own differing concepts of biblical history because nothing in her studies even remotely suggested that Jesus was less than divine.

Anne recalled her first interest in the scriptures and found it amazing that she used a Bible given to her as a child.

Lilly, her adoring baby sitter and self-appointed grandmother figure who worshipped the ground she walked on, had given her the gray hard cover Catholic Bible when she was about ten years old. She had also given her sister one just like it.

Anne marveled realizing that was the Bible she had available to her when she decided to read the scriptures some thirty years later!

Anne had traveled the country, attending dozens of different schools after her father's death when she was only four years old and her sister was two. Her mom remarried a man from out of state and they moved west to the farmlands of Oklahoma leaving the cold snowy Illinois weather behind. His work took him to many different states and they followed along.

Looking now at that familiar Bible, color coded from years of study, Anne realized what a miracle it was that she happened to still have it thirty years later when she decided to read it.

As much as Anne disliked traveling as a child, she found her new life with Al thrilling. Their travels from earthquake to blizzards, hurricanes, tidal waves and floods were filled with adventure. Anne followed Al from one end of the country to the other and so did that Bible.

Just as interesting as the different places they visited, were the books that seemed to present at the right time for Anne, as she was learning new and interesting biblical facts.

Her favorite book appeared on a shelf in an antique store somewhere in the Citrus counties of Florida one Sunday. She and her husband had gone to church, dined out and then browsed the local stores. The pretty dark blue book with gold lettering entitled *The Forgotten Books of Eden* captured Anne's interest. Al purchased it for her and Anne found exciting answers to questions that had presented while studying the scriptures.

Her first impression she recalled while studying both the Old and New Testaments was the strangely strong feeling that Jesus had been here before. The many mentions of his rising again made her question when he had risen the first time.

Over the years Anne had learned that every question that presented to her was answered if she diligently sought it. She knew from experience that if you knocked it would open, if you would seek you would find, and if you asked it would be given. She had full confidence in the power of God, the divinity of Jesus and the knowledge conveyed by the Holy Spirit. She also knew that as one mystery was solved, another would rise up to keep her tantalizingly interested in knowing more and more about the spiritual mysteries of God.

Again, the idea of the divinity of Jesus being called into question brought her to the realization that she should indeed read *The DaVinci Code.* This question was one that cried out to her, and she knew she would be given the answers.

A few days later she secured the book and lost herself in the story. Dan Brown was an artist as a writer. Each page was filled with elaborately descriptive detail and immediately Anne found that she was an avid fan of this remarkable writer. The story was intriguing and this was one of those rare books you couldn't bear to put down.

When she finished she was exhilarated. Her ideas changed immediately from being judgmental about the book, to being intrigued about the story of the Magdalene. She still couldn't see Jesus as a married man, but there was something to this story, and she was determined to get to the bottom of it.

She learned that the Magdalene story had been translated from old papyrus scrolls that were uncovered in the last century and finally translated. This, in and of itself, intrigued Anne because she had found so much information from ancient stories in her own spiritual studies.

She was on a mission to know the truth! In Anne's experience, the books would always appear when she needed the information they had to divulge and she was in a position to better understand the message. Just like the first book in Florida appeared to her at the right time, she knew beyond any doubt that she was on a new adventure in mystery solving.

The DaVinci Code referred to another work entitled *Holy Blood, Holy Grail*. This book was apparently the first to relate the Magdalene secret. It provided an in depth study of the Magdalene, tracing the possible genealogy of her bloodline down through the ages. It also gave an account of those entrusted with the secret and their endeavors to maintain and protect the supposed holy, royal bloodline. It told a fascinating story of Mary Magdalene being secreted away by boat to France after the death of Jesus, where she gave birth to his daughter.

The Magdalene story staggers the conscience of a devout mind. It has concurrently drawn forth a distinct variety of beliefs, myths, sects and assumptions that have shrouded the Magdalene in secrecy for centuries, which when combined with an investigation into the matter advances just as many opinions and theories as to its significance.

Like oddly configured pieces of a puzzle coincidentally fitting together to form a picture, the extraordinary story of Jesus continues to expand and develop as pieces of this centuries old puzzle emerge from antiquity to shed new light on the man heralded as the Messiah, the Son of God, the Son of Man and the Christ. Enticing and intriguing bits of information issue from depths of old like drops of oil forming rainbow colored circles on the water's surface.

Therein lays the challenge that presented when Anne made the decision to find her own truth about the Magdalene. Like a swimmer approaching the shores of an ocean, she took one step after another until an overwhelming flood of information swelled like a wave and plunged her into new depths of learning while raising her to new heights of understanding. The excitement that ensued was unmatched by any previous spiritual experience as the pieces of the puzzle began cascading into place, forming a picture she had neither dared, nor could have begun to imagine.

CHAPTER THREE

Sunday after Thanksgiving was a beautiful day. Anne was so thankful that her mother's health had returned after two long years of a debilitating stomach disorder. She had actually eaten and enjoyed dinner at Michelle's on Thanksgiving. The dinner was a huge success and everyone had a good time.

Anne used to cook the family dinners, but passed the mantle to Michelle the year she moved to the country. Anne started a new tradition that evolved into quite a fun evening the night before Thanksgiving. She called it the *breaking bread and wine party to stuff the turkey* because that's just what it was. This past Thanksgiving party had brought together a nice variety of friends and family - just the girls, of course. Michelle was especially excited because she had just purchased her dream stove!

Her cousin, Christy, arrived that evening and Michelle showed her the huge stainless steel stove with five gas burners and two electric convection ovens.

"I told my girlfriend that you had a dream stove and she said, 'I have had a dream car, a dream home and a dream boat, but I never had a dream stove!"

Everyone chuckled over Michelle's excitement for her new stove.

"Well, it really is my dream stove! I love to cook and I learned how to cook on a gas stove when I was growing up. All I have ever had since then are electric stoves. I could spend all day cooking on my new stove. It is a dream come true."

"I know. You go to something cooking dot com to get new recipes!" her cousin teased.

Anne had always been very close to her niece. She was like an older sister to her own daughter. Michelle and Christy was a pair of beauties to behold and Anne adored them both.

Christy bore a thick curly mane of long golden brown hair that framed huge beautiful blue eyes that sparkled with humor and compassion. She had the lithe slim figure of a ballerina, and dancing had played a prominent role in her life.

She started dancing at age five and had majored in dance at college. Whenever she performed she brought down the house. Anne's favorite memory was when Christy competed in a beauty pageant during her college days. She performed a tap dance to a dramatic Broadway musical version of the song, *Sweet Georgia Brown.* Her spectacular red costume was highlighted with gold sparkle and set off by a large red feather boa that draped from her shoulders to the floor framing her slim figure and beautiful dancer's legs.

The song began slowly with Christy casting a dramatic side glance into the audience. That *look* captivated them.

She then walk-danced through the first steps of the opening - until boom! The tempo broke into a dazzling drumbeat and she tossed the boa onto the floor and launched into her dance. Her shoulder length mane of curls swirled and the audience watched spellbound as her rapid fire taps propelled her around the stage in a breathtaking dance that eventually slowed when she picked up the boa, and ended with that *look*!

The explosion of applause was no surprise to Aunt Anne - *that girl had it*!

Christy went on to compete in a world competition in New York where she placed in the top five and won a scholarship to a theatrical school. She was offered an audition for a national football team cheer leading squad. Instead of pursuing her dancing career, Christy married her childhood sweetheart, opened her own dance studio and became a wonderful mother to three most delightful, beautiful and talented children of her own.

Anne and her mother thrilled to Christy's dances and their dream of seeing her dance again never waned. They knew she was destined to perform.

Christy was especially close to her grandmother and never missed a day calling to check on her. They shared a common deep grief in the loss of Christy's mom, her grandmother's beautiful blonde baby whose death came too soon. The bond between Christy and her grandmother was sealed in their mutual loss and love.

The family was very close and there were never any secrets. Michelle, Christy, Anne and her mother always knew every detail that went on in each others' lives. It was a running joke that anyone who confided a secret to one of the others was whistling in the wind, because each confided to the other. They would laugh because they knew there were never any secrets in this family.

Anne was spending that restful Sunday studying and writing a little. She noticed that her attention was curiously drawn to the family and that was the new thread that was weaving its way through the fabric of her book. She seemed consumed with the story of the Magdalene lately.

She is a saint so I should pray for her to help me discover the truth.

As soon as she thought about this she made a special intercession to the saint for help in understanding the mystery that surrounded her.

I need your help and there is not much biblical information to study other than the few times you are mentioned in the New Testament.

Immediately, two Old Testament Books came to mind: first was the book of *Ruth* and then the *Canticle of Canticles.* She smiled to herself as she picked up the familiar old Bible that morning and recalled how everything she ever learned was always confirmed to her in this book.

You are my special guide, she thought fondly as she opened her Bible and began to read. She was happy to be reading it again because she had laid it aside for the past few weeks to read another New Testament book that was rendered from the original Greek. She had found interesting new insights in it, but her old gray tattered Bible was her favorite companion and friend.

Anne again thought about the interesting way certain

books always came to her that held special information and the timing of their arrival was always perfect in her spiritual learning process.

Al had brought her this New Testament book from an estate sale recently.

Actually, Al has played a significant role in bringing many books to me. He took me to that shop in Florida where I found The Forgotten Books of Eden.

Al had brought home the book, *Holy Blood, Holy Grail,* years earlier, but she hadn't been interested in it at that time. Then, after reading *The DaVinci Code,* she needed that book! She smiled recalling Al having shown it to her so long ago. She didn't have to search for it very long because she found it in the first place she looked. There it was waiting for her on a shelf at the top of her closet.

Anne wondered at the magical way information was brought to her. It was while she was thinking about her own special Bible as the very important book that completed all of her own stories in one way or another that she was struck by another thought from her distant past.

Anne was taken back in time when she and her sister were about 6 and 8 years old. Their mother had hired a lovable big, black woman to take care of them during the day and her name was Ethel Mae.

Oh, my. I haven't thought about her in ages.

She laughed to herself as she remembered Ethel Mae and her brother taking her and Marcia to the park in a small Oklahoma town to hide Easter eggs.

When the black couple appeared with a little blonde and redhead, the park seemed to empty itself of inhabitants while they played and had a good time. Thinking back she realized how odd they must have appeared at that time and place. Of course, it hadn't been remarkable to her or her sister. They were completely unaware of racial prejudice in their childish innocence. What stood out about Ethel Mae though, were the stories she would tell the girls every time she came to stay with them.

"Oh! Ethel Mae! Where do you get all those wonderful stories?" they would ask.

And she would tell them, "I have a great big book at home."

"Ethel Mae, will you please bring that big book so we can see it?" Anne remembered begging her as a child.

Later, Mother told her how Ethel Mae would laugh and say,

"Those girls think I have a great big book full of stories, but I just make them up. There really isn't a big book!"

Anne saw her own story book growing faster than she could write it. Now she had to put the facts to paper and allow the story to unfold exactly the way it was presented. There were still pieces of the puzzle that were forming, but she knew the end was very close.

Where do I begin to tell such an amazing story?

She decided to report it as it happened which unfolded like a diary of events. It all began when she started writing her fourth book earlier this year. *Trust Me* was the name she had been given for this book, and that is exactly what she did. She knew it was not her book, she was only the scribe.

CHAPTER FOUR

Anne's Journal -- January 2003

I had just finished self publishing my first book *A Spiritual Trilogy*. In it I elaborated on the spirits of error and the spirits of God that I had found in the lost or ancient Book of Reuben. The spirits of God consisted of senses and one power as I counted them. My favorite was the power of speech. Of all the spirits of God, this one was listed as a power. At least that was how I had understood it for years.

One day shortly after publishing my book, I was shocked to find that I had missed a second power in the list of the Spirits of God. It was the Power of Procreation.

> *Seven spirits therefore are appointed against man, and they are the leaders in the works of youth. And seven other spirits are given to him at his creation that through them should be done every work of man.*

Testament of Reuben, Ch. 1 vs. 12-13.

The Spirits of God - and - The Spirits of Error

1 Sense of Smell	Insatiableness
2 Sense of Sight	Fighting
3 Sense of Hearing	Obsequiousness & Chicanery
4 Sense of Taste	Pride
5 Power of Speech	Lying
6 Life	Injustice
7 Power of Procreation & Sexual Intercourse	Fornication

This oversight stunned me. *There were two spirits with powers! I had missed one. How did this happen? How could it stay hidden for so long?* I wondered.

I had copied the list down for my personal use, and my list was missing a very important power! I know nothing can remain hidden forever. Everything eventually comes to the light - and how delighted I am to find this information. I also believe spiritual information is conveyed only when I am able to understand it.

This information was surely necessary for my ever increasing knowledge and spiritual growth.

Knowledge of these spirits has played a major role in my personal spiritual journey. A path that began in spiritual darkness and extended into the spiritual light of God's love revealed wonderful mysteries along the way, and the path continued to take me to new heights of understanding as it illumined the area surrounding me.

The best known spiritual journey is that of the Israelites fleeing Egypt for the Promised Land as recorded in the Old Testament. There is no doubt God was with them in the desert providing food, shelter, clothing and protection along the way. Yet, when it came time to enter the

Promised Land, they didn't make it in. The path ended short of the promise because they failed to trust God.

Their spiritual journey ended because their focus was turned from spiritual to physical circumstances. They resorted to their physical senses, rejecting the spiritual gifts of God. They ran in terror from giants. Instead of standing their ground and trusting God they ran in fear of man. *Trust Me* may sound like an easy instruction, but this age old story proves the difficulty one encounters at the entering into the promises.

It takes unswerving dedication and unfailing faith in an invisible God to stare down a giant that looms in your path. Only after one has fully developed the inner spiritual man does he find the courage and strength to relinquish the control of the physical man.

The Western mystic saint, St. Teresa of Avila, described the surrender of the flesh man to the spiritual man in a beautiful and serene way: L*ike a dewdrop slipping into the shining sea.*

Trusting God is the complete surrendering of rational emotions wrought with fear. The opposite of fear is faith, and spiritual growth cannot be hurried. Indeed, you do not send an infant into battle. The flesh and blood body came first, the spirit second. One must decrease as the other increases.

I often wondered why it was such a struggle until I understood where the battle was taking place. The battle is not with God. It is a battle within our very self, between our ego and our spirit. The ego puts up a terrific fight while holding onto emotional bondage in its determination to stay in control.

Some have an easier transition than others, but that is not something we can blame on God. We are each different in our strengths and weaknesses because we are free agents with the freedom to choose.

I feel it is important to elaborate on the importance of spiritual development, because it is definitely a work in progress.

There have been times along my own spiritual journey when I wondered why God didn't just "do something" for me. Of course, I have wondered why there should be trials and sorrows when it would be so easy for God to fix everything!

Here is the catch! I cannot go to God in the flesh. God is spirit, truth and love. God is there for me all the time in spirit. He has given me the power to choose and, therefore, I understand that unless and until I make the decision to surrender my limited physical control and allow God to take over in his unlimited spiritual power, I will continue the struggle.

The age old struggle is always between faith and fear. My desire is to develop that inner spiritual person that is able to trust God, and surrender my control. The struggle is with my own flesh. God will not overturn my decisions!

So, if I struggle it is because my flesh is fighting for its very life. Trust is the key that unlocks the door to spiritual promises.

Slipping into the shining sea doesn't describe a crash or even a splash. No, rather it is a quiet, peaceful experience. Surrender is a letting go of ego and willpower, and discovering that God can do it so much better when we allow Him.

At this stage of my spiritual development, I am discovering much to my delight that I can't do it all, I don't want to do it all, and I rejoice that I can surrender all my desires to His will. Once that dewdrop mixes into the shining sea, the outcome is not only one of submission, but of empowerment. We become one with God, and our will becomes His. Only after a journey and battle with our own desires, do we discover that His ways are indeed higher and purer than we can accomplish in our flesh. His will is our will after all. The fight we had along the way was finding out that important truth.

So, let's enter in and find what treasures He has in store. My discovery of the power of procreation is timely indeed. For I am excited to discover God's powers working within me.

I learned the importance of the power of speech in bringing forth positive or negative circumstances based upon our spoken words. Now, I am impressed with the importance of the thought that goes before the words. The power of procreation is just what it describes - it is the power to create.

Of course, procreation is the producing of offspring, but that is only the physical attribute. The deeper or spiritual importance of procreation is the creativity it contains. God is the Creator - this gift staggers the mind with the potency of its power! Think about creativity. It gives birth to all of the arts. Music, writing, painting, and dancing are all forms of creativity. The pictures that are formed in our imagination, which can be limitless, can be brought into being by our spoken words.

It is very important that we develop our power of speech to express positive words rather than negative. And, more importantly, we should develop our imagination to see positive images that are limitless in possibilities. The mind is a wonderful artist, and through the power of procreation we can create our dreams with our imaginations and give birth to them by the power of our speech. That is the significance of the two spiritual gifts of God that are described as power.

God spoke and there was light. God creates with His word, and here we discover that God has given us the power to create with our speech. It is a twofold process. First, we must imagine our desire, and then we should speak it. The manifested power of God is available to those who become one with Him.

Shortly after discovering the power of procreation, I re-read the Story of Enoch in, *The Forgotten Books of Eden.* Enoch was the seventh son from Adam who pleased God and was taken up to Heaven. In this ancient story there is a dialogue between Enoch and God when he is taken up to heaven. God shows him the many levels of heaven, the hierarchy of the angels and the wonderful workings of the seasons. This story also relates that Enoch was given to write many books.

God then sent him back to earth for a short while to share his knowledge and books with his children. Then, God brought him back to heaven.

During their conversation God tells Enoch how He imagined and perceived the world and those things that He created before He spoke those famous words *"Let there be light!"*

While reading this discourse, I was struck by the very fact that God talked about imagining the sun or the moon and then creating them. He also used the word perceived in describing what he saw before speaking something into existence.

True to form, when I seek I find. The power of procreation which, of course, is for the very purpose of the regeneration of mankind, was also shown to me in the broader sense.

Not only do we produce in the flesh, we also produce in the spirit. The power of procreation as listed in the spirits of God is a spiritual gift imparted to us for spiritual creativity. In the spiritual sense we have the power to imagine or create images in our mind that can be brought forth or manifested into the physical realm. Everything God created in tangible form was first imagined and perceived in the intangible.

This is a very exciting revelation of the power to be able to create. The very powers God employed to create are within us! God brought forth visible things from invisible things. Therefore, if we can see it in our mind, we can speak it into existence! The two powers work together!

The spiritual power of procreation is limited only by our own imagination, or enhanced by it.

Inspired by the revelation of the power of procreation, I enhanced the prayer of Jabez and prayed:

- ❖ O, *Lord, that you would bless me indeed*
- ❖ *and enlarge my territory –*
- ❖ *enlarge my receptacle to receive your blessings*
- ❖ *that you would expand my imagination*
- ❖ *that your hand would be with me*
- ❖ *to keep me from evil*
- ❖ *that I may not cause pain –*
- ❖ *and I cast down all the limitations I have placed on you, Father*
- ❖ *that I may receive the full blessings.*
- ❖ *Open the floodgates and pour out your blessings*
- ❖ *fill my receptacle to overflowing*
- ❖ *let me experience my destiny in you*
- ❖ *let me be encompassed in your love, your beauty, your light and your music*
- ❖ *and perform your will not mine*
- ❖ *In Jesus' name - I pray. Amen.*

CHAPTER FIVE

Anne understood the information that she had learned about the power of procreation was another piece to the unsolved mystery that was unfolding in the story of the Magdalene. She also understood the vast chasm between physical and spiritual realities, and how the thread of similarity eventually would weave itself into a blanket of understanding.

She had a mystery to solve. She was about to be taken on a new spiritual adventure and she could not stifle the excitement that was smoldering in her soul.

The joy of solving a mystery is a reward to the senses. It is a knowing of things you just can't quite put your finger on.

Anne believed that mystery-solving was a unique quest in every individual. It is a person's very nature to search for answers to the many wonders that present. We seem to spend our lives wondering and asking "why."

There is a thrill in solving mysteries and finding answers to life's many questions. Life itself is the mystery and God is the Creator of all living things.

Ah, sweet mystery of life.

The very questions rising up from one's depths bring the realization that the answers themselves will be found in that same mysterious depth. Oh, maybe not at first. Initially, one searches the world for answers, but eventually the senses are awakened to new skills of perceiving and understanding, and that is when man discovers his other self. This is the beginning of spiritual awareness, and it is thus, by the spirit, that seekers are led into the desert to begin a journey to the waters of spiritual knowledge.

Anne knew that her answers were not necessarily the same answers as another. Each person must reconcile themselves to God in their own time and their own taste.

Taste is a sense, and it is unique to each individual. A spiritual challenge is to taste and see how good He is. Each man must discover his own truth and it begins with a taste for spiritual knowledge.

Taste is that spiritual gift which is employed to sense the power and goodness of the Lord. It is in this sense of taste that Anne understands the diversity of religions. A wide variety of ideas compose religious thought and so various religions appeal to a variety of spiritual tastes. Not all desire to expand their palates to include exotic dishes. Choice is a God-given right imparted to man by God. Anne found many aspects to God that were diverse and exciting and she understood this to be the basis for our own diversity.

Anne couldn't shake the need to defend the divinity of Jesus and that was the motivation that drove her to probe the story of his marriage, and the resultant theories that maybe he was just an outstanding prophet or good man. She knew, beyond any doubt, the Holy Spirit would show her the truth. She opened up to embrace new ideas about him that she believed would not fail to maintain his divinity, regardless of the outcome. She was excited to learn what the Spirit had to reveal to her on the subject of his marriage.

While *The DaVinci Code* was a fiction, the Magdalene story was found written in ancient documents. The fact that ancient papyrus scrolls were translated to reveal this story struck Anne's heart. Her spiritual journey had been sprinkled with lost manuscripts and ancient stories. These very stories contained the information that broadened her understanding of God and brought sense to the Bible stories that were missing information. Together the information had blended to form the basis for her greater understanding of Jesus.

The mystery of Jesus rising again was the first question that she committed to prayer for an answer. She got an answer too, and that answer is what prompted her writings years ago. The story that was given to her about Jesus did not disturb nor diminish his divinity, but it certainly added a whole new dimension that only she could understand. That was why she had to write the story, it was too wonderful to hide, too large to contain, and, she recalled, identifying it with *The DaVinci Code,* too controversial to share.

That book had struck a chord and signaled to Anne that it was time to share the mysteries she had discovered. It had opened the door for this story and prepared an audience who was anxiously awaiting the answers that were being revealed to her about the controversial marriage of Jesus to Mary Magdalene.

She knew that her first book was just the groundwork for the one that is forthcoming. Her study of the mystery of Jesus had provided the basic understanding required to solve this new mystery.

Anne believed beyond any shadow of a doubt that Jesus was the Son of God, and she had a broader knowledge of his person. She documented her new understanding in an elaborately detailed account in her previous book. In order to tell the new story she would have to first explain the findings that were the result of her earlier studies.

Without rewriting the detailed intricacies of her former book, Anne believed these facts to be true of Jesus. First, she believed he first appeared on the earth in the person of Abel. This belief stemmed from the account of God speaking to Eve in the garden when He said to the serpent, *"I will place enmity between your seed and her seed."* God's seed is His word. Jesus is God's Word. And, Anne believed God placed the seed of Abel at this instant when He spoke about the enmity between the seeds of Eve.

Second, she believed that God took Abel into heaven after Cain murdered him, and there trained him to break the gates of brass and bars of iron that he was destined to do when he returned in the person of Jesus, overcoming spiritual death and setting the captives free.

Third, she believed that he would come again for the final battle as described in the Bible. This was the Jesus she understood and knew to be the divine savior of the world. He was the only Son of God, but she believed he had appeared on earth twice and his next appearance would be the third one instead of the second.

This was how Anne knew Jesus and her commitment to his divinity as the Son of God and the Son of Man was unshakable.

Thinking one day about the absurdity of Jesus being married, she stopped in her tracks as she remembered the account of Abel's murder that she had read in the Story of Adam and Eve.

This ancient story gave an account of Adam and Eve when they came out of the garden. It was much more detailed than the one given in Genesis and it made sense.

This story revealed that Cain and Abel were each born with a twin sister.

Cain's sister was named Luluwa which meant beautiful because she was more beautiful than her mother. Adam named him Cain which meant hater because the story said he hated his sister in their mother's womb.

Abel had a sister named Aklia. When the children were teens their parents decided they should marry and they planned for Abel to marry Luluwa, Cain's beautiful sister.

The story then tells of Satan coming to Cain and telling him that his parents loved Abel more than him and that was why they wished to join Abel to his beautiful sister, Luluwa. He told Cain they hated him and wished him to be married to the ill-favored sister.

The marriage of Abel to Lulawa planned by Adam and Eve became the motivation for Cain to murder his brother.

Anne was astonished that she was praying about the truth of the marriage of Jesus and she was being shown that the first murder was committed over the marriage of Abel; the man she believed was Jesus.

CHAPTER SIX

Anne's Journal -- July 31, 2003

Yesterday marked the day that St. Thérèse (also called "St. Theresa" and "The Little Flower") was anointed before her death. She then lingered and suffered through September. I finished re-reading her book the night before and my eye was drawn to one of the last words she had written in ink, before resorting to the pencil. It was italicized and I recalled that any word that Theresa had capitalized or underlined had been italicized in this book.

The word was restlessness and she was describing the story of Martha and Mary, when Mary sat at the feet of Jesus while Martha was busy about the supper preparations. Theresa said it was God's will for us to not have restlessness. The italics on that word meant this was important, so I looked up the word and then I understood her message to me was to rest.

Funny, that her message today is for me to rest, since I believed she had caused me to clean like a maniac all day in my kitchen. I moved every piece of furniture and the refrigerator to clean behind it. Then, noticing how much brighter the floor was behind this furniture, I was moved to buy two brushes and scrub the grout and the tile on my hands and knees. This task had taken several hours. I was very tired when I went to bed - and now she says I need rest. *Well I guess so, Theresa!*

My mother had called last night when I was nearing the end of this task. I laughingly told her I had been possessed by a saint and I was scrubbing the floor on my hands and knees like a monk or sister would do in a monastery!

After I wiped the last tile, I stood and gazed on the beautifully bright white floor and felt such a surge of joy that I began singing. As the verse came out - I stopped and gasped, *"No!"* I was singing, "Everything's Coming up Roses!"

Roses! It is you Theresa! My favorite saint, the Little Flower, has certainly captured my soul. I just re-read her book the past few days and marveled at all the similarities between us. She even used the word ravishing - and Mom always teased me about using that word. She wrote her book in three segments - *so did I! S*he wrote them over the course of three years - - *so did I!*

Oh, I have believed the words that I grew up praying in the Apostles Creed: *I believe in the Holy Ghost, the holy Catholic Church, the communion of saints . . . . And now it is coming to pass. Indeed, Theresa is communing with me spiritually. It is such a wonderful spiritual experience, knowing that I have a saint in heaven watching over me, guiding and teaching me.*

The more I understand this communion, the more I stand amazed. Who is Theresa, but the Rose? And who am I spiritually, but a vase! A vase to contain the rose! Only God in His almighty wisdom and power could bring about such a wonderful communion as this.

First, He gave me my new name, Anne Urne, (an urn - a vase), then He revealed my patron saint who is none other than a rose.

It was a most astonishing recognition as I discovered who had pushed the pencil in my hand twenty years ago when it wrote on my tablet: *"lousy world, better love now."*

Last year, when nearing the end of my work on *A Spiritual Trilogy*, I discovered the western mystic saints. St. Thérèse, my patron saint, was one of them. I immediately found and read her book, *The Story of a Soul*. I learned that she was unable to finish her book because she was dying of tuberculosis. She was a Carmelite sister who at age 24 had written one of the most famous spiritual books of the ages.

Comments by her older sister, also a nun at Carmel, explained how the last few pages had been written by Theresa in pencil as she was too weak to hold up the clumsy pen. She further explained how the last words trailed off and only a scribble was left where Theresa fought to keep writing because of her strong will, even though she was so weak and coughing up blood and dying an excruciating slow death of suffocation. Thérèse desired to die a martyr's death, and so she did. She suffered exceedingly before departing to be with the Lord.

Twenty years ago in my deepest darkest depression ever, a psychic co-worker had told me that I had a spiritual guide who was a woman with dark hair. She explained that this guide would help me. Immediately, when I returned to my office in a state of great despair and hopelessness, nearly mad with grief, I prayed and asked my guide, whoever she was, to please help me.

I didn't know which way to turn or what to do. As I was praying, I had a pencil in my hand and a yellow tablet on my desk. I was alone in my office when, to my astonishment, the pencil began to gently move across the tablet. The words appeared which I will never forget - *lousy world better love now.*

While reading St. Thérèse's *Story of a Soul* I learned that her vocation was LOVE. She is the beautiful nun whose picture I admired as a child which showed her holding the crucifix surrounded by roses. She was known as the Little Flower. That was all I knew about her when I chose her as my patron saint at my Confirmation at age twelve.

Now, I know her intimately and I understand that she has been the guide who has been with me since my youth. She is so important to me. My saint prophesied before her death that she would come back to save souls for Jesus at the end of the world, and that she wanted to spend her life in heaven doing good on the earth.

To understand the communion of saints is nothing short of spiritual development and I rejoice that my spirit is growing and that my growth is guided by such a dedicated and loving saint. How wonderful God is to send us saints and angels to help us in this world. How much greater to begin a spiritual development that brings us closer to the realm of heaven, where we can learn the secrets that saints know, and to understand the depth and heighth and length and breadth of God and His love for us.

St. Thérèse of Lisieux is my very own, beautiful patron saint. She vowed to come back to help save souls in the end times and has been credited for many miracles and is especially known for helping soldiers during World War II. She is my inspiration and my friend.

It is through her famous "little ways" that I have found the answers to the puzzling dilemmas that life seems to "spoon up" on more than one occasion.

Ever since I learned my prayers in Catholic school, I have countless times recited the Apostle's Creed, and never wondered what it meant when I prayed, I believe in the Holy Ghost, the holy Catholic Church, <u>the communion of saints</u>, the forgiveness of sins, the resurrection of the body and life everlasting. Amen.

Not until I became aware of the presence and help of my own wonderful saint, did I realize that I had confessed the belief in the communion of saints my entire life. So, what is communion? Of course, I only thought of that word in terms of the sacrament in which we partake of the bread and wine. Not until I discovered that my saint is undeniably present to help me, did I consider what this portion of the prayer might really mean.

I looked up the word communion searching for the true meaning of what I had been confessing all of these years.

Here is the treasure-trove of words I found to describe communion: exchange, union, fellowship, agreement, sharing, association, togetherness, intimacy and familiarity.

So, the communion of saints means to have an exchange with them. It means to be in union and fellowship. Better than that, it is an intimate and familiar sharing. I am a better person because of my communion with this saint, and I beg the skeptics to pause and not confuse the communion of saints with psychic mediums or Old Testament tampering with the dead.

God's children are saints and when our loved ones pass from here, we pray that God will receive them into his kingdom with the saints who have gone before. When I speak of communion of saints, let me be emphatic about this point, I am not speaking of contacting the dead! Saints are alive, because Jesus overcame death and to commune with them is to learn the very secrets of sainthood.

The saints provide enlightenment and understanding and, even better than that, they love us. They couldn't help but love us because they are living in God's love.

To pray for help from the saints is no different than seeking professional advice from a doctor when we are sick or a clergyman when we are in need of counsel.

I have found that sometimes life presents problems that seem beyond our capacity to solve. In these times of distress, the help of a saint can assist us in obtaining the miraculous answer or cure. A saint's advice is truth.

Just as there are two sides to every story, so is there a spiritual view versus a natural view. Who could be better than the saints who have gone before us to help guide us into the light of proper perspective? Who could be closer to God to lift us up in prayers?

The words of wisdom imparted to me by my saint so many years ago were simple and true. At the time, however, I did not know who gave me these words:

LOUSY WORLD BETTER LOVE NOW.

It was 1983 when I was given these words. In 2003, I found the author and the understanding. Yes, it was St. Thérèse, my very own patron saint. She has been with me through all my ups and downs. As I take my spiritual journey to a new level, I am delighted to have found my very own communion of saints with the saint who has kept a vigil over me since the day I chose her to be my patron at the young age of 12.

Now, I wonder why I took so long to discover the truth. The answer is simple. I was young, I was strong and I could do it all my way. Only, when I learned that I can't handle the whole load, did I learn what it meant to surrender myself to the Lord. The help of a saint brought me the information and guidance I needed to find relief for my weary soul.

Now, I can rejoice when I am weary, for then I am strong in the Lord. It is true what Paul and John taught in the scriptures about rejoicing when we are weak, for the Lord is strong. It is all about the two people we are in this world, until, like Christ crucified, we become one.

Surrender is the sweetest, most victorious, joyous and freeing sacrifice one can make. Surrender sounds like defeat, but it is a relinquishing of fleshly desires that opens the door for the inner spiritual man to surge to the forefront in invigorated strength. Like a long held air bubble below the surface it rises in power and explodes on the surface in the renewed strength of God-given power!

With this renewed strength, knowledge, joy and peace you understand, at last, the difference in giving and taking. The tables are indeed turned, as we look at the futility life held for us in the flesh, because now you see and understand the power of the man that has been held captive below the surface of your life.

Jeane Dixon described the devil as one who takes by giving. That describes the nature of the flesh as we know it. It is easily seen in the example of using a credit card. It seems to give us something, but its purpose and usual success is to take back many times more than it gave.

God teaches us to give. This is the law of the spirit of truth. The difference between spiritual and natural law is easy to perceive. God's giving is for receiving not taking. God instructs us to give without expecting a return. The spiritual truth of giving and receiving is the very truth of God. He gives to us and yearns to give to us, but we must receive what He offers. Hold out your hand to God and let Him fill it. The part we have such difficulty grasping, is receiving what God is giving us. The precious gift, of course, is Jesus. When we can receive and believe, the spiritual well will overflow into eternity.

The communion of saints is a wonderful experience and it leads to deeper and greater understanding of God who is love, through His Son and His Holy Spirit.

Anne's Journal--August 5, 2003

You are weak and tired. It is time to rest. Why is it so hard? My pastor gave a sermon on rest this Sunday, and I knew - it was time to write this chapter.

Emerging from a recent forced rest after a near bout with stroke, I find that it is with much difficulty that we exercise our will to enter into the rest. I heard the inner voice speak to me very clearly that I should rest.

Scriptures illuminated my understanding that in peace and calm we inherit the promises. So, I forced myself to lie down, read and meditate in the book of the prophet Isaia. I have always found that my spirit soars to new heights when meditating in this wonderful book, and I was not disappointed. After feeling downcast in spirit and being brought to a physical low by a stressful work environment, it took an act of faith to even rest from the multitude of thoughts that raced around aimlessly in my head. Rest seemed to be hiding from me by the mere distraction of my reeling mind.

After making the decision that I would rest, I went to my room and lay on the bed. After reading for about an hour, the book slipped down and my eyes closed. In a wake-like dreamy trance, I sensed the approach of a large bright blue bird with a green breast - big and beautiful. It came and sat just above my left shoulder. I knew that it was going to climb onto my shoulder and that I must remain quiet and calm. Certainly, this large bird gave me pause and a tinge of fear, but I didn't breathe. I closed my eyes and remained quiet and calm. Gently the bird stepped up onto my shoulder.

Oh, this was something special I knew as I opened my eyes to the empty bedroom. It was indeed a spiritual manifestation and it meant something. Just this week Christy told me her story of the humming birds. God is sending us humming birds and blue birds of happiness. What did God do when Jesus came up out of the water, but have a dove descend on him? The bird is significant of the Holy Ghost descending upon us and that means the anointing is here!

I rejoice indeed! For the thing I believed, to step off into the spiritual realm, has manifested - now it comes to pass!

The wonderful appearance of the bluebird gave my spirits a well-needed bounce. Now, my mind was singing Zippity Doo Dah, what a wonderful day. Mr. Bluebird's on my shoulder!

Now, I truly understood the wonder of peace and calm. Only in that state would a bird step onto my shoulder. Any sudden movement or alarm would have spirited the bird away quickly. But, I rejoiced that I had succeeded in peace and calm. This was a spiritual victory, indeed.

I have since resumed my old routine of doing temporary work in law offices, and I shudder as I witness so many young attorneys working at a frantic pace from dawn until late night to crank out more work. More work, more billing; more billing, more money. The whole frenzied work place gives me butterflies and feelings of sorrow for the poor souls trapped in these work camps. How long before they discover the wonder of peace and calm so they can enter into God's rest? Somewhere there must be a balance established between work and rest.

My pastor preached a whole sermon on the fast paced environment we exist in. He stressed the importance of God's commandment to rest on the Sabbath. Along with the exhortation to rest one day out of seven, he set forth an important message that it is not the particular day, such as Sunday, but rather one day - any day of the week.

The importance of rest is not the day, but the rest itself. This was enlightening as it was a confession of the spirit rather than the letter of the law. Of course, being a minister, he couldn't take off work on Sunday! So, he set aside another day and called Monday his day of rest.

CHAPTER SEVEN

Anne's Journal--October 18, 2003

My spirit was in flight this morning, and I had dreams of travel and shopping. I called Christy to tell her about it.

"I was flying, too!" she told me when I spoke to her.

"I dreamed I was in a large room with a massive fireplace with a mantle. There was no fire in it, but I had a pot of water and I poured it into the hearth. After doing that, a liquid with things in it began flowing out, and it filled my pot. I had to get more and more bowls to catch it."

"I saw things in the liquid, so I reached in and pulled something out. It was an ember. I laid that in the fireplace and first it glowed. Then, it started a fire! Fire and water! And this was an altar - because during it all, I was seeing the face of Jesus which had appeared over the mantle. He was speaking to me the whole time. Then, he put his hands on my cheeks and kissed my face!"

"Oh! Christy, how exciting! That's wonderful."

"It was awesome and significant of spiritual fire and water!" she continued.

Christy was a joy to talk to and her spiritual perception was very keen. She was a spiritual prodigy in my book. Later, I spoke to Mom and just had to tell her about Christy's dream. Remember, this is the family that can't keep any secrets. I had to laugh when I told Mom that Jesus kissed her face, because she didn't miss a beat responding.

"Who WOULDN'T want to kiss Christy?"

Anne's Journal--October 19, 2003, 3 A.M.

I thought about writing, and I remembered how Christy put in a little and much flowed out. That was my inspiration as I started to write today, believing that if I put in a few words, He would pour more out on the pages. And this morning, my theme is "The Five Assumptions". Give me your words Lord, as I return to my new book.

Well, it worked. I have the most exciting chapter I have ever written and an extraordinary revelation about the Seventh Assumption! This chapter was a powerfully emotional victory.

THE SEVENTH ASSUMPTION

* * * * * * * * * * * * *** * * * * * * * * * * * * * * * * * *

Growing up in the Catholic Church, I have always believed in the Assumption of the Virgin Mary. This is a belief that the Church has maintained down through the ages. It appears that most of the Protestants left this assumption behind as they blazed new trails of independence from the mother Church.

Obviously, the belief of the Assumption of Mary is, indeed, an assumption. The Bible gives us no verbatim verification of this miraculous event. Assumption is described by Webster as:

1.   The taking up of a person into heaven; specif. [esp.], the taking up of the Virgin Mary; also, a church feast (August 15) commemorating this.

Webster continues with three more definitions, with the fourth being the act of taking for granted. And, the Church most assuredly takes for granted the Assumption of Mary.

Interestingly, in my first book *A Spiritual Trilogy,* I was given to write about several "assumptions" - five, to be exact. I will enumerate on these after explaining the more commonly known assumptions which are the two that are recorded in the Bible.

The first recorded assumption was that of Enoch, the seventh descendant of Adam, who pleased God and was taken up into heaven.

The second recorded assumption was that of the Old Testament prophet, Elijah, who was seen taken up to heaven on a fiery chariot.

After reviewing these biblical assumptions, it came to my attention that I had written about five assumptions which included the two above, but my writings didn't go into detail about Mary's Assumption.

So, as I added the Assumption of Mary to the number of persons that I believed had been taken up to heaven, the count now became six assumptions.

This count, in and of itself, gets me very excited. Let me try to explain without getting too far ahead of myself. You see, seven, is the perfect number of God in which all things are perfected. So, this perfect number seven is realized when we add the last return of Our Lord when He comes on the clouds to take up all the saints into heaven. This truly becomes The Seventh Assumption!

The Seven Assumptions that I have been given to understand are in this order:

1) Abel;

2) Eve;

3) Enoch;

4) Moses;

5) Elijah;

6) Mary; and

7) The Seventh Assumption.

Christians would be familiar with the biblically published assumptions of Enoch and Elijah. Catholics believe in the Assumption of Mary. The others on my list require more explanation.

In my earlier book I wrote that I believed Moses had been taken up into heaven. The scripture that aided me in this particular belief came from the New Testament Epistle of St. Jude where it was written: "Yet, when Michael the archangel was fiercely disputing with the devil about the body of Moses . . ."

Much to my surprise and joy, I read something just the other day that spoke of an old Jewish tradition and a book called *The Assumption of Moses*! Joy, indeed because this means that I am not alone in my belief in the assumption of Moses.

It seems, then, that among some Jews, Christians and Catholics we can find a common thread of belief in four assumptions; those being the assumptions of Enoch, Moses, Elijah and Mary.

Now this brings me to the assumptions that were given to me through inspiration, or better described as spiritually imparted to me. These would be the assumptions of Abel and Eve.

In an attempt at brevity, I shall touch on the reasons that I believed in the assumption of Abel. This occurred while I was deeply involved in a personal study of the Bible. Certain biblical passages enlightened me. Then, I stumbled upon obscure manuscripts of ancient stories of creation. Finally, the whole picture came together in an almost mystical type of knowing that is sometimes referred to as a conviction. I knew beyond any doubt that Abel was created by the word of God and brought into being. Then

God took him up into heaven and trained him for his return in the person and name of Jesus, our Savior.

The psalmist best describes my belief in the assumption of Abel (known as Abel the Just) after he was slain.

> *The breakers of death surged round about me, the destroying floods overwhelmed me; the cords of the nether world enmeshed me, the snares of death overtook me.*
>
> *In my distress I called upon the Lord and cried out to my God; from his temple he heard my voice, and my cry to him reached his ears. . . .*
>
> *He reached out from on high and grasped me; he drew me out of the deep waters. He rescued me from my mighty enemy . . .*
>
> *The Lord rewarded me according to my justice . . .*
>
> *The God who girded me with strength and kept my way unerring; who made my feet swift as those of hinds and set me on the heights; who*

trained my hands for war and my arms to bend a
bow of brass.
Psalm 19

This is only one of many scriptures that led me to my belief that Abel the Just was the Son of God who was taken up to heaven.

Some years later I came to understand that Eve was the pure creation of God who was not tarnished by original sin and, therefore, she was the pure mother of God's child, Abel. From my studies of Eve and Mary, I concluded that they were one and the same. God brought Eve back into heaven until it was time to return her to earth in the person of Mary. Being the only creation of God who had not fallen out of grace, the Angel Gabriel said to her, "*Hail, full of grace, the Lord is with thee. Blessed art thou among women.*"

The following scriptures and excerpt from *A Spiritual Trilogy* are provided here for clarification about my belief that Eve and Mary are one and the same, and that both had an assumption:

> *And a great sign appeared in heaven: a*
> *woman clothed with the sun, and the moon*

was under her feet and upon her head a crown of twelve stars. And being with child, she cried out in her travail and was in the anguish of delivery. And another sign was seen in heaven, and behold, a great red dragon having seven heads and ten horns, and upon his heads seven diadems. And his tail was dragging along the third part of the stars of heaven, and it dashed them to the earth, and the dragon stood before the woman who was about to bring forth, that when she had brought forth he might devour her son. And she brought forth a male child, who is to rule all nations with a rod of iron, and her child was caught up to God and to his throne. And the woman fled into the wilderness, where she has a place prepared by God, that there they may nourish her a thousand two hundred and sixty days.

Apocalypse 12: 1-6.

And when the dragon saw that he was cast down to the earth, he pursued the woman who had brought forth the male child. And there were given to the woman the two wings of the great eagle, that she might fly into the wilderness unto her place, where she is nourished for a time and times and a half time, away from the serpent. And the serpent cast out of his mouth after the woman water like a river that he might cause her to be carried away by the river. And the earth helped the woman, and the earth opened her mouth and swallowed up the river that the dragon had cast out of his mouth. And the dragon was angered at the woman and went away to wage war with the rest of her offspring who keep the commandments of God, and hold fast the testimony of Jesus. And he stood upon the sand of the sea.

Apocalypse 12: 18.

Reading these scriptures only intensify my belief that Eve brought forth Abel, the Son of God, "*who is to rule all nations with a rod of iron; and her child was caught up to God and to his throne. And the woman fled into the wilderness . . .*" Eve disappeared for a time, and I believe that was because God brought her back into heaven. Then, we read again that the dragon was angered over the woman who had given birth to the male child. I believe this refers to the birth of Jesus, and this scripture then describes the dragon going away from the woman angry to wage war with the rest of her offspring who keep the commandments of God, and hold fast the testimony of Jesus.

Excerpt from *A Spiritual Trilogy.*

My studies and meditation brought me to a complete confidence in my beliefs that Abel, Eve, Enoch and Moses were taken up to heaven where God prepared them for their return. The mission of these persons in their two earthly visits are, again, detailed and recorded in the former book which defines each person's integral role in the salvation plan. This plan that was instituted by God at the very moment He sent Adam and Eve out of the garden.

The number of assumptions becomes most remarkable when you add the one that is imminent and find the total to be seven which is God's perfect number. There is no doubt in my mind that there will be a Seventh Assumption!

This very wondrous spiritual revelation shines a light on Jewish, Catholic and Protestant beliefs. However, in order to understand the entirety and wonder of the revelation, there must be the consideration of the spiritual or unseen factor that resides quietly, just below the surface, waiting to manifest itself to those who seek the answers to God's wonderful mysteries. This magnificent revelation is perfected in the final assumption. Perfectly, the saints are gathered together and raised into heaven at the Seventh Assumption!

The revelation of the Seventh Assumption brings with it a very dramatic climax. The perfect number seven is realized in the prophesied phenomenon, called by some, the rapture. And oh, how marvelous and complete my joy becomes at the very realization that God has shown me a new name for this extraordinary event, being The Seventh Assumption. The crescendo of my excitement bursts into inexplicable joy because I know that a new name is significant of a spiritual name!

> *He who has an ear, let him hear what the Spirit says to the churches: To him who overcomes, I will give the hidden manna, and I will give him a white pebble, and upon the pebble a new name written, which no one knows except him who receives it.*

Apocalypse 2:17.

Anne's Journal--October 19, 2003, 10 P. M.

Later on the same day that I had written the chapter on the seventh assumption, I was plagued by a nagging thought that I hadn't included Jesus in the list.

I wrestled emotionally over this thought. It was a roller coaster of emotions from the heights of bliss over the revelation of the seventh assumption to the dashing disappointment that loomed in the foreground of my mind. If the assumption of Jesus was added to my list, the seventh assumption would no longer be!

I had to think this through. I couldn't imagine that the information I had received could be wrong! I prayed and asked God to show me the truth, for nothing but the truth would satisfy my anguishing soul at this moment.

Spiritual learning is something that is given to you in a holy inner conveyance. The very fact that it is a spiritual knowing of a certain idea, conveyed through scriptural study, prayer and meditation, brings with it a glow of inner joy. The verification of a spiritual conveyance by way of some kind of witness brings an even warmer glow and understanding that is beyond description. It is literally putting your finger on something that before was hidden. It is a manifestation of an unseen spiritual truth. Trust me, it is exciting.

I was in the middle of a spiritual quandary, no doubt about it. I certainly could not deny that Jesus was taken to heaven, but I also couldn't grasp that the seventh assumption was incorrect. This was a struggle between my spiritual and mental acumen, and I always chose the spiritual over my mental capacities. I knew that doubts, worries and negative thoughts came through the mental processor, whereas the peace and assurance that bubbled up from my spiritual depths was a reassuring knowledge of truth. I also found that each truth was verified by a witness of one type or another that eliminated any doubt from deterring me from my belief in its veracity.

My dilemma was complicated in that I was convinced of the correctness of the seventh assumption and even believed I had received a type of witness to that number.

After finishing the chapter, I had time to get ready for church. I looked forward to church and prayed the Holy Spirit would bring me a wonderful word from God during the service.

Expecting must be emphasized right now, for unless we are looking and expecting, we miss the treasures that God sends to us by various means. Again, I was not disappointed in my expectation. The sermon was on forgiveness, but the scripture was about forgiving 7 times 70. There was the confirmation of my seven assumptions. Seven was the truth!

So what happened to cause the struggle that afternoon? A thought came to mind that could change the number seven that I had been so sure was the correct number of the assumptions. I was home alone that day and fixed a wonderful brunch for myself after church. Still thinking about the assumptions and recounting them in my mind, I suddenly remembered that Jesus was taken up and I hadn't even listed him in my count of seven assumptions.

Oh, the disappointment sunk in as I wondered how I could have missed it.

I went back to my computer and began trying to rewrite the entire chapter to include Jesus and searched for ways to justify eight. I began writing and referring to my previous book where I had written about the significance of eight days and tried to make eight come out sounding correct. I succeeded to some extent, because I knew that eight was a significant number when counting the days for I had written about that, as well, in my previous book. I finished re-writing the end of that chapter, then left to take a walk.

It was a picture perfect day in October with the temperature hovering in the low 70's, a cloudless bright blue sky and leaves turning to red and gold as I walked my usual mile long trek through the neighborhood. The birds sang loudly and I felt good.

At the end of that day, before going to bed, I picked up the blue hard cover New Testament my husband had just given me and began reading. There, on the second page of the introduction, my eyes fell on the word "Ascension."

The flood of understanding broke out in a hallelujah chorus as I stared at that word Ascension. Of course! Jesus rose into heaven on his own power because he is God. His rising up to heaven was not an assumption where one is taken up. His was ascension because he took himself up on his own power! You can well imagine the excitement and indescribable joy that erupted in my soul. My mind raced to catch up with the overwhelming understanding that resolved my inner conflict over the number of assumptions. There was the confirmation of my spiritual knowing that the resurrection of the saints was truly The Seventh Assumption.

I did not go to bed until I had put the chapter back into its original form. My new Bible had become a trustworthy friend and I was looking forward to reading it from cover to cover.

CHAPTER EIGHT

Anne was flooded by the memories of her previous studies that had led her to believe that certain special persons had appeared on earth more than once.

She was being shown how her earlier revelations of these persons were forming the foundation for her higher understanding of the mystery about the Magdalene.

Anne often wondered why she had been convinced over a decade ago that Jesus was Abel. She believed this beyond any doubt, but wondered what difference it made. She seemed to be the only one who knew or cared to know this interesting concept. It didn't change the salvation story of Jesus, so the significance of her inner conviction seemed insignificant in the overall picture.

Anne's revelation of Jesus and Abel had shown her how the Son of Man, Son of God, had overcome two deaths. She believed that the assumption of Abel into heaven was significant of him overcoming physical death as the Son of Man, and the Ascension of Jesus into heaven was the overcoming of spiritual death as the Son of God. Jesus is described in the scriptures as overcoming the enmity in the flesh and making the two one. She understood this to mean that Jesus had made the two men, the spiritual man and the physical man, one complete and perfect man.

Now, this information was being shown to her as the very basis and link for solving the mystery that presented to her about Mary Magdalene.

Her initial repugnance to the story of the marriage of Jesus was fierce. This story was being bantered about by the arrival of the controversial book, *The DaVinci Code.* Anne didn't even want to read a book that contained such a blasphemous allegation about her Savior.

There was something about her friend's suggestion to read *The DaVinci Code* that kept tugging at her

Trust Me ♍ 101

---

conscience. After her initial negative reaction to shun the book, came her resultant positive response to read it for the sake of defending the truth about the divinity of Jesus.

Anne knew from past experience that the truth cannot remain hidden. Her life was a continual feast of spiritual mysteries that were being revealed as she pursued new heights of spiritual enlightenment. She was being challenged to find the answer to a question that could only be answered spiritually.

Surprisingly, the book won Anne's heart. Never had she read anything as exciting and well written as this book. Her immediate affinity toward the author made it impossible for her to be upset with him for sharing the story of the marriage of Jesus and the Magdalene. He did it with style and grace and provided the information as it truly presented from long lost pages. He referred to the book *Holy Blood, Holy Grail* for a source of information.

Anne's intrigue heightened at the challenge of this mystery presenting to her. She knew it was not just a coincidence that she happened to already be in possession of this next book. She wasted no time locating the book that had been sitting idle and unread on a shelf in her closet for many years. Now, it was time to read this one.

There were facts presented in *Holy Blood, Holy Grail* about the secret societies that had existed for centuries who were dedicated to protecting the story and purported offspring of Magdalene and Jesus. Anne found some of the beliefs of these secret societies to be puzzling and contradictory. They tried to humanize Jesus in order to present a sensual man capable of marrying and fathering children; while, in the very next sentence, they described the blessedness and holiness of the Magdalene and her offspring of Jesus!

How can she and her offspring be described as holy and blessed - unless Jesus is divine? Where is the sense in this?

The story of Mary Magdalene continued to unfold in remarkable sequence as Anne persisted in getting to the heart of the matter.

Her initial thoughts about Jesus being two persons opened the doors to new insights about his mysterious relationship with the Magdalene. The constant doubt that Jesus was ever married stemmed from her own idea that Jesus, as a divine entity, would not be able to marry a human who had the stain of original sin. In keeping with her personal Christian beliefs and understanding, all humans had inherited the stigma of original sin that had been passed down from Adam throughout all generations.

There were, however, some exceptions that Anne had noted in her previous studies. She especially believed that Abel was conceived by God's word. The son of God born to Eve was the same person Anne knew as Jesus who was conceived by the Holy Spirit and born of the Virgin Mary.

In fact, Anne also believed that Adam was the one who suffered the sin of spiritual darkness by disobeying God and eating the apple. Anne believed that Eve was deceived by the devil, but she was not guilty of the sin of disobedience to God's command that had been given to Adam prior to her existence. As a result, she maintained a new found idea that Eve was the only possible means for God to bring a human into the world that was undefiled by sin.

The salvation plan was implemented just before Adam and Eve stepped out of the garden. Anne's understanding of this mystery was that Abel was the seed of God born by the pure person of Eve, and that God took both of them to heaven to await the fulfillment of time when they would return in the persons of Mary and Jesus. The purity of these two souls was undeniable in Anne's understanding.

The key to solving the mystery of the marriage of Jesus presented quite a challenge to Anne and the timing seemed to be out of place. She was busy composing her new non-fiction book, *Trust Me*. This book was emerging as the result of her deeper spiritual insight, and now it was taking a new turn in its development. The tantalizing information about the Magdalene that had been disseminated through the vehicle of a fiction murder mystery gave her pause as she pondered the possibility of doing the same. The idea of being able to concoct a murder mystery as a vehicle to launch new spiritual insights into an age old mystery of the Magdalene loomed discouragingly into her thoughts. How should she proceed with this book in light of the new discoveries that were presenting at the same time.

How ridiculous! I may have a vivid imagination, but never in my wildest dreams could I conceive the makings of an intricate murder mystery.

She wrestled with the work she had before her and finally decided that her new book should be written as a fiction that would allow the reader to assimilate according to his own taste the wisdom contained within the pages.

Much to her surprise, the answers that were coming to light as she probed the story of the Magdalene brought her smack into the middle of the first murder ever perpetrated on the earth!

Oh my goodness. There IS a murder mystery that I can write about! Anne thought in astonished surprise.

Of course, discovering the murderer is not what constitutes this mystery. He was known from the outset. Everyone knows that Cain murdered his brother, Abel.

This murder mystery is not about the murderer, it is about a marriage and the fate of a family affected by that murder!

Now, she understood the significance of her beliefs about Abel. It is this very revelation that was propelling Anne into a remarkable mystery that begged to be solved.

Before she would be able to tell the story of the Magdalene, she first had to know the story of Abel. She saw the glimmer of light shining in the distance that contained the truth of the story of Magdalene and her marriage.

As rapid as the speed of light, the information was presenting itself in a colorful spectacle of reflection and new information. There seemed to be an urgency driving and guiding Anne to each new tantalizing piece of this puzzle. There was no denying the unveiling of this mystery. Its birth was imminent and the story that was evolving was incredibly believable.

Anne felt as though she was holding her breath as she anticipated the next insight. She could hardly wait to see the complete picture that was forming in the near distant light.

She determined to organize this new information that was flooding her thoughts as she sat down with the book that was already in progress. The task appeared overwhelming, until she was reminded that she alone cannot tell this story. She is only the scribe.

She shook off the anxiety, took a deep breath and proceeded; one word at a time, to present the story as it unfolded to her.

It all began when she was driven by her determination to defend the divinity of Jesus. After all, the very suggestion of sexuality being linked to Jesus triggers the question of his divinity. Either he is human or he is divine. Sexuality lends to humanity and hence distracts from divinity.

Thus the question of Jesus' sexuality was the first and most formidable obstacle to piercing the veil of truth. The only acceptable answer that she would entertain would have to come from the divine, Himself. Hesitatingly and with apprehension, at first, then with an honest zeal for truth she posed the question in prayer to her heavenly Father.

She knew from experience that He never failed to show her the truth in all her endeavors and learning. She had been studying and writing about new spiritual truths for many years, so this was not a new approach. She had every confidence that God would show her the truth about the marriage that so plagued her mind for an answer.

She placed her question as a prayer on the invisible table, left it, and expected to receive an answer. Attempting to explain spiritual acumen is a difficult proposition. It has been termed gnosis by some, revelation by others, spiritual imparting, significant coincidence, and insight by others. It is the knowledge that comes from within. The explanation of a spiritual understanding can be a struggle to bring the semblance of rationale to things that aren't necessarily rational. The knowing from within is reflected in the scriptures of Jesus speaking in parables, because some were just not able or ready to understand. There is a reality in heaven that is distinctly different from earthly reality. However, it seems to offer a mirrored type similarity to the reality in earth.

Within days of Anne's prayer, she was figuratively stopped in her tracks by a thought that came out of the blue and could only be described as spiritually audible.

"Jesus was described as two! He was Son of Man and Son of God."

Anne's own conviction was that Jesus had made the two men one in his sacrifice on the cross. She understood that he sacrificed his humanity to become united to his divinity, and this gave credence to the possibility - just the possibility at this point - that the humanity of Jesus, and not the divinity of Jesus, might possibly explain the conflicting information about him and the Magdalene being married.

This could possibly explain the myriad of confusing and conflicting opinions about whether or not Jesus was truly divine. Never had she been drawn away or enticed by any suggestion that Jesus might not be divine.

Anne's desire was to know the truth that would prove the divinity of Jesus and put an end to the allegations that he was only human. The conspiracy of the secret societies that protected the secret of his marriage to the Magdalene became a worse conspiracy to humanize the divine. The secrecy of this marriage seemed to spawn conflict and confusion between the idea of Jesus being human and his offspring being royal.

A light had sparked Anne's conscious awareness of Jesus being two. Now she was being shown the struggle that ensued in trying to explain the two persons of Jesus. There was something about to be revealed in this message that came to remind her that she already knew there were two. The two were Abel and Jesus. The two were human and divine!

The human man died in the sense that he was no longer human, but rather complete and divine as the Word of God and Son of God. The Son of Man took on the sins of man in the flesh in order to restore mankind to its spiritual identity. This is how the mystery began to reveal itself. Over the forthcoming weeks and months that Anne devoted to this study, more astonishing information shed light on this age old mystery.

CHAPTER NINE

"Hello, hello." Anne couldn't wait to tell Michelle more about the amazing things she was learning about the Magdalene mystery.

"Hi, Mom, what's new with you?"

"I'm glad you asked. I am getting so much information about the Magdalene."

"What's the latest?"

"My attention is being remarkably drawn to the subject of marriage. Remember the dream I had about you about a month ago when I dreamed you got married?"

"No."

"Oh, how could you forget? It was very funny. I dreamed that you married your husband's brother, and then I told you that you would really have a dysfunctional family!"

"Mom, I don't remember that."

"Well, actually it was pretty silly at the time. But, now it makes sense to me."

"Why, Mom?"

"Because my study of Magdalene 1S about a marriage."

"Well, if you think it's important, that's fine. I just don't recall you telling me about it. There is no way I would be marrying anyone other than my husband. He is my perfect soul mate. I knew that from the time I first met him. We have always shared the same dreams and enjoy the same activities."

"There's more! Yesterday, I reviewed my book that I have been neglecting too long - and guess what?"

"Okay, what?"

"It is so astonishing! The first chapter began with another dream about marriage. You see, it all comes together! My book started out with a mystery about a marriage before I ever stumbled upon the mystery of the Magdalene marriage. I can hardly contain my excitement over the book that was waiting for the rest of this story. Here I was wrestling over how to incorporate the two stories, and the book was already prepared and waiting!"

"Well, Mom, you and I already know how wonderfully God leads us into new areas of understanding. I'm glad your book is coming together.

I don't understand the bits of information you keep giving me, so I'll just have to wait and read it when you're finished."

"Oh, you will understand it all when it's finished. I know it! You have a great day."

It is no wonder Michelle couldn't follow the many and various trails that Anne had chartered over the past weeks. There seemed to be so many, but they were all culminating onto one path.

In *Holy Blood, Holy Grail,* Anne read that some disputed the authorship of the Gospel of John. Anne was surprised to learn that nowhere in that Gospel was the name John ever mentioned. Instead the author referred to himself as the disciple whom Jesus loved. This Gospel commented on how dearly Jesus loved Lazarus. He even wept at his tomb.

She quickly re-read the Gospel of John and found it was true. This book is referred to as the spiritual Gospel. Anne found this new revelation remarkable, and it was weaving itself into the picture that was forming about Mary Magdalene, the sister of Lazarus and Martha.

The pieces of the puzzle were found in a variety of books and the pattern was formed in the place where knowledge is imparted. From apocryphal books, biblical books, fiction, nonfiction and ancient papyrus scrolls, the picture was coming into focus. It was a family portrait of old: the first family of creation!

God created man in his image. In the image of God he created him. Male and female he created them.

God spoke to the serpent in the garden before expelling Adam and Eve. He said, "*I will put enmity between you and the woman, between your seed and her seed . . .*" Then, he spoke to the woman saying, "*For your husband shall be your longing.*"

Anne believed that Cain and Abel were spiritual beings planted before Adam and Eve came into the world of humanity, and she believed that the *longing of Eve for her husband* was reflected in the fact that his spiritual light had gone out. She believed that Eve was able to return to heaven, but Adam could not because of the darkness that had settled onto him for his disobedience. Adam was destined for captivity after his death, but Anne believed that Eve was able to return to heaven because her soul was not darkened.

Adam and Eve were originally one until God created Eve from a rib he took from Adam's side. The Book of Genesis describes the birth of two sons, Cain and then Abel. It then leaves us in the dark about how these two sons begat the next generations for there is no mention of any other persons on earth at that time.

Many years ago, Anne found a collection of ancient stories and apocrypha in a wonderful book entitled, *The Forgotten Books of Eden.* She delighted in these stories and they propelled her along on her pursuit of spiritual growth and knowledge.

Here is where she found, *The Story of Adam and Eve.* This story told that Cain and Abel were each born with a twin sister. Anne believed they were spiritual beings who originated in the spiritual realm before being born in the earth.

Genesis records that much later Adam became the father of a son in his own likeness, after his own image and he called him Seth.

This reference to Seth served as a confirmation to Anne that the other sons were different - spiritual. A son of light and a son who chose to follow the ruler of the darkness of the world.

Anne never gave much thought to the sisters of these men until recently. While considering the possibility of the marriage of Jesus, she was immediately reminded of the murder of Abel.

Abel and Aklia, being brother and sister, were of the same seed. They were the seed of God, and appropriately created male and female. Aklia was the female counterpart of the same seed of Abel.

Cain was the first son born in the world and he also came into the world with a twin female counterpart, named Luluwa. Her name meant beautiful. Cain was described as having red hair.

The story told of the sons growing into teenagers when Adam and Eve planned their marriages. They decided to marry Abel to Cain's sister, Luluwa. It was at this point of the story that Satan came to Cain and stirred him to jealousy over the marriage of his beautiful sister to Abel. Cain became very angry and decided to murder his brother so he wouldn't be able to marry his sister.

Anne was being shown that Abel, whom she believed to be the same person as Jesus, had been deprived of his marriage. This information evolved into Anne's understanding of the marriage of Jesus.

The first family on earth consisted of Adam and Eve and their five children: Cain and Luluwa, Abel and Aklia, and Seth.

After Cain murdered his brother Abel, the story relates that Luluwa heard the words spoken between Cain and God and went to tell her parents of the murder of Abel. They brought Abel's body back to the Cave of Treasures where they mourned and cried over him.

Cain came and took Luluwa away without his parents consent for they were too weak with grief to prevent him.

Seven years later Adam became the father of Seth. When Seth came of age, his parents married him to Abel's sister, Aklia.

All of the children were married except Abel who died. Abel was to have been married to the girl that Cain kidnapped. Anne realized that it was justice for Abel, returning in the person of Jesus, to indeed marry! She also understood that the Savior was both human and divine.

First he was born into the world of flesh as Abel the Just, who Anne identified as the Son of Man because of the place of his birth being in the physical world. Then he returned from heaven as the Son of God who was called Jesus.

Was it possible, then, that Jesus returned as both persons, the human and the divine, to complete the marriage that had been deprived him in the first instance?

There was more to learn and Anne had prayed to Mary Magdalene to help her find the answer. She wanted to know more, but was unable to find much about her in the Bible other than the few references to her in the New Testament. Much to her amazement, Anne was directed to two books from the Old Testament. Immediately after she prayed to Mary Magdalene, these books flashed in her mind, *Ruth* and *Canticle of Canticles.*

First, she read the *Canticles* and marveled when she read where the bridegroom called his lover, *my sister, my bride*, not once, but over and over. Anne had not dared to conclude that Jesus had married his sister, but there it was in her favorite Bible – '*My sister, my bride!*'

Which sister she wondered? But she knew. It was the sister of Abel, and the twin of Cain. The beautiful bride was one and the same beautiful Luluwa who was chosen to marry Abel!

Anne quickly turned to the story of Ruth and found even more treasures. Here she discovers a widow who was taken to a foreign country with her husband and two sons. The sons had both married in this foreign land and now they and the father were dead. The widow was left with just two daughters-in-law. Anne immediately recognized these women as Eve with Aklia and Luluwa who had married her sons.

Interestingly, in the book of Ruth, the mother returns with one daughter-in-law and this girl marries a prominent relative of the mother. She is married into the family of the ancestry of David!

The confirmation of Anne's understanding of the marriage of Jesus was confirmed in her favorite book of all, her very special Bible.

She turned again to the *Canticles* and read more surprising and confirming scriptures. The bride saying to her lover, "*Oh, that you were my brother, nursed at my mother's breasts.*" In another verse she said, "*I took hold of him and would not let him go till I should bring him to the home of my mother."

Anne read these verses as Luluwa speaking to Abel. She wished she had been his twin, and she would not rest until she was returned with him to her mother. She called herself a lily of the valley and the bridegroom replied, "*As a lily among thorns, so is my beloved among women.*"

Luluwa was the beautiful sister who was stolen away by her murderous brother to live among the thorns of the world.

The *Canticles* shows the bride searching desperately for her bridegroom and warning others "*do not arouse, do not stir up love before its own time.*"

Anne saw this warning to be the result of the murder and kidnapping that was perpetrated in a rage of passion and jealousy. Love had been stirred up at the wrong time for Abel and Luluwa.

Another verse that stood out in the *Canticles* was the Bridegroom saying, "*Under the apple tree I awakened you; it was there that our mother conceived you.*"

Confusion stirred in Anne as she tried to relate to the spiritual and physical realities of the original family and their destinies. She had learned that Seth married Aklia.

She also understood that Seth being the true child of Adam was also born into the state of darkness and captivity. He would not be able to enter heaven until the Savior came and released the captives.

Anne again studied the Gospel of John and found remarkable scripture that brought greater clarity and understanding to the mystery of Mary Magdalene. Now she was studying the Gospel as if it were written by the disciple that Jesus loved. That disciple was Lazarus. This shed a whole new light on the scripture.

The Gospel of John is the only one that tells of the marriage at Cana. It is also the only one that tells of the raising of Lazarus. This Book contained the information that pointed directly to the children of Adam and Eve. Here Anne found Martha, Mary and their brother Lazarus. By now, Anne was seeing that Mary Magdalene was the sister of Abel and the twin of Cain who had been kidnapped. Remarkably, Mary Magdalene is found in this scripture with a sister and brother. If, as Anne was discovering, Mary Magdalene was really Luluwa, that would make Martha and Lazarus none other than Aklia and Seth!

An eruption of knowledge spewed into Anne's consciousness as she recognized what Jesus had done by raising Lazarus! No wonder Jesus wept at his tomb! This was his brother whom he had not lived to see in his first visit to earth as Abel. This was the brother who took the place of the lost son, Cain. It was stressed that Lazarus had been in the tomb four days. God's time is one day to a thousand - and it had indeed been four thousand years since Seth would have died on the earth and gone into the captivity of darkness. The raising of Lazarus was nothing less than the dramatic restoration of Seth!

The final scene at the cross was even more dramatic when Anne read the following lines:

Seeing his mother and the disciple whom he loved standing by, Jesus said to his mother: *"Mother, this is your son."* He then said to the disciple: *"This is your mother."* That same hour the disciple took her into his home.

Anne understood that the original family was being restored.

All, except one, were in that book. Cain was the odd man out. The five children were now four and they were standing in the presence of their mother.

Jesus restored the children to his mother prior to his death. Then, as it is written: *"He descended into hell."*

Beginning with his father, Adam, Jesus released the souls that had been held captive and brought them into Paradise.

Anne had found more information than she was able to comprehend at one time. The bits and fragments came together perfectly. Then, one night before finishing her writing about the Magdalene, she ran across an interesting television program that was discussing biblical mysteries. She learned there was a Gospel of Mary Magdalene. She knew she had to locate a copy of this gospel and she prayed to all the saints and to the Lord for that book. She found it the next day.

CHAPTER TEN

Anne could hardly contain her excitement. She called Christy to tell her.

"Christy, you're not going to believe this. I have found the most exciting information yet in my study of Mary Magdalene. It is above and beyond my wildest dreams. I can hardly form the words to describe the excitement and joy that has been stirred up in me."

"It goes back to a number of things. First, of all remember how we always knew that your Mom left us with the legacy to imagine?"

"Oh, yes."

"You also remember when I told you about overlooking the power of procreation and how important I believed that was?"

"Yes, Anne, I do."

"Well, that was left out of my last book and so I put it in the beginning of this new book."

"Anne, I remember when you started that book. I also remember that your spirits were down when you were recuperating from your bout with high blood pressure."

"I remember that!" Anne exclaimed

"I told you then that you needed to be writing."

"Oh, yes, Christy. You are the dear who said you were proud of me for writing and publishing my own book. You encouraged me even though I felt I had failed since I didn't know how to market and sell it."

"I do believe you accomplished a great thing by publishing your own book. I also know that your joy is in your writing," Christy continued.

"I'm so glad you encouraged me to write again, because this book has taken me to such heights that you just can't imagine!"

"Tell me your exciting news."

"I found the Gospel of Mary Magdalene!"

"That is terrific!" Christy understood and shared Anne's enthusiasm.

"And it is just so fantastic! The narrator of the book described her message as one of CREATIVE IMAGINATION!"

"Wow!"

"You understand the importance, don't you? I mean, that was what I had interpreted and written about the power of procreation. I believed that power was conveying the importance of imagination and creativity working together to accomplish and manifest our dreams."

Of course, Christy understood. "That is remarkable. I'm glad you are so happy, Anne."

"Yes, I am very happy and it is time to collect all this information I have gathered and write it down. I'll talk to you soon."

Anne hung up the phone and danced with joy. What better witness to her understanding of the Magdalene than the Gospel of Mary Magdalene, herself!

She read more of the Gospel and found that Mary Magdalene was described as having red hair.

Of course, she had red hair! She was the twin of that redheaded Cain!

Anne smiled as she recalled her own mother telling her for as long as she could remember that redheads were special -- because Anne was a redhead.

You, Mary Magdalene, are truly special!

You were the grieving sister who cried over the body of Abel. You were the woman who cried at the feet of Jesus and anointed him for his burial. You were the one who knew of his imminent death.

It is said that Jesus drove seven demons from you. Of course, those would be the same seven spirits of error assigned to every man that are listed in the Book of Reuben. All of us came with the same seven. But Jesus, delivered you, married you and made you whole.

You found the way to that place between spirit and body where one communes with the saints. You maintained communication with Jesus after he departed the earth

Yes, yours was the wedding at Cana. You are indeed the bride and sister of the Lord. Your marriage was the perfect union of male and female and it marked the end of the separation that began when Eve was taken from Adam.

> *God created man in his image.　In the image of God he created him.　Male and female he created them.*

Gen. 1:27

And when God brought Eve to him, he said, "*She now is bone of my bone, and flesh of my flesh, she shall be called Woman, for from man she has been taken.*"

The union of Mary Magdalene and Jesus marks the restoration of the only divine man and divine woman, both being of the same bone, flesh, blood and parentage of the first perfect creation.　The perfect bloodline - together - the very image of God!

EPILOGUE

The study of Mary Magdalene brought a renewed understanding of the meaning of her appearance at this particular time in history. First and foremost, she was signaling the importance of the restoration of the family.

Secondly. from her Gospel it can be learned that she knew the way to the place where she could see Jesus.

The Gospel of Mary (speaking to the Apostles) page 10:

7   Mary said to them

8   "I will now speak to you

9   of that which has not been given to you to hear.

10   I had a vision of the Teacher.

11   and I said to him:

12   'Lord I see you now

13   in this vision.'

14   And he answered:

15   'You are blessed, for the sight of me does not disturb you,

16   There where is the nous, lies the treasure."

The place where she was able to visit was called the nous. Continuing in the next verses from this passage, Mary asks the Lord where this place is located.

17 "Then I said to him:

18 'Lord, when someone meets you

19 in a Moment of vision,

20 is it through the soul that they see,

21 or is it through the Spirit?"

22 The Teacher answered:

23 "It is neither through the soul nor the spirit,

24 but the nous between the two

25 which sees the vision, and it is this which . . .

[Pages 11-14 are missing]

Mary was able to see Jesus in a special place after he had departed from this world. Somewhere between the soul and the spirit is another realm that is very real and it is in this place, called the nous, that the living can commune.

Anne rejoiced over the little book that evolved this year. Each year since 2000 she had produced a small book that was completed each year right at Christmas.

Happy Birthday Jesus - and thank you for the wonderful new book. Today is Christmas and it is finished.

Anne approached Christmas filled with anticipation, and excitement knowing beyond any doubt that her book would be completed in time. And, it came to pass. She reached another Christmas and had completed another book.

In January of this year she had published her first three books in *A Spiritual Trilogy* and hadn't anticipated writing another one this year. The self-published book seemed to be the culmination of a long work and it also seemed to signal the end of her writing. She had learned so much over the past decade and it all was contained in those books.

She was motivated by her wonderful niece to write again this year. Christy explained that she was only happy if she was writing - and she was so right! The fulfillment derived from writing these books go way beyond the physical realm of joy. It is a pure happiness that comes from within.

While anticipating the close of her latest book, Anne began to wonder about the book cover. She thought of using a picture of a cross and roses like the one held by her famous St. Thérèse. She believed the roses to be symbolic of Mary Magdalene and the cross, of course, was symbolic of Jesus.

Anne couldn't help but speculate about the little St. Thérèse who was from France. That is the place where it is believed Mary Magdalene was hidden with her child. Anne wondered, was St. Thérèse an offspring of that branch of the family?

She looked in Thérèse's book to find the complete name that she took upon entering the convent.

Interestingly, she found where St. Thérèse, to amuse herself, composed a letter of invitation. It began thus:

Letter of Invitation to the Wedding of Sister Thérèse
of the Child Jesus and the Holy Face

She called herself of the Child Jesus and the Holy Face. A very interesting and tantalizing name she chose. Was she signifying that she had descended from the child of Jesus and knew the place where she could see that Holy Face? St. Thérèse is my very dear and special saint who guides me in more ways than I am aware. Her significant presence originally led me to consider placing the cross and roses on my first publication. Instead, a much better picture emerged to grace the front cover.

The picture of the Crystal Vase made the perfect cover for Anne's first published book. It held great significance to Anne. It represented her new name Anne Urne. She understood the representation of herself as an urn - a vase.

The Crystal Vase used in the photograph was also very special. It was a gift from her husband that took center stage in a gold lighted cabinet in their home. The vase symbolized the container that Anne had become for the indwelling of the Lord. That vase had caught Anne's eye at the Farmer's Market in Los Angeles while she patiently waited for Al to shop among a room filled with bronze statues. The vase was in the back of the store, high on a shelf, and it sparkled at her. She knew she had to have this beautiful vase – and Al bought it for her.

Anne had read another wonderful book by the western mystic, St. Teresa of Avila, just before completing her Trilogy. St. Teresa wrote about the soul being like a crystal palace in her book, *The Interior Castle.* This was yet another confirmation of the symbolism of her Crystal Vase.

Now that she was approaching the end of her new book, she couldn't help but wonder about the cover.

The more she thought about the cover, the more she favored using her beautiful vase.

But, somehow, it must be different this time, she thought.

Then, she saw it-- with roses! Three to be exact. One for the Holy Virgin, Mary; one for her patron, St. Thérèse of Lisieux; and one for St. Mary Magdalene.

That's it! she decided happily. That vase with three roses would be perfect on the cover of her latest book.

On Christmas Eve, Anne went to Michelle's house to begin preparations for the Christmas dinner. They cooked all afternoon on the dream stove. Then, she rushed home to get ready for a candle light Christmas Eve service at their local church. Al greeted her as she dashed into the house tearing off her clothes. She had only fifteen minutes to get changed and ready for church! But, Al had something on the table for her to see. She turned and followed him to the dining table.

Oh, look!

He had bought her some flowers. And – there, on the table stood a vase containing three roses!

* * *

Have you ever wondered how some people just seem to

know things?

Words from the Author:

This book was left unpublished for three years. Then, on St. Patrick's Day, 2006, I traveled to a seminar to see a featured speaker and author. I had just recently discovered this Magdalene scholar and read several of her books.

Towards the end of this two-day seminar I experienced a most wonderful and dramatic spiritual event. It happened during a brief meditation period and slide show presentation of beautiful Mary Magdalene paintings while soft music played. We were told this melody had been inspired and composed for Mary Magdalene. During this brief meditation with a room full of spiritual seekers, the speaker suggested to the audience that, if they were so moved, they might wish to write a short verse. She suggested one that possibly would begin with one word, then two words, three words, four words and then end with one word.

As the music began playing softly and the slides displayed beautiful paintings of Mary Magdalene I was overcome with emotion. Tears began bathing my face and I was helpless to stop the flood of tears while gazing upon the beautiful Magdalene. Much to my surprise a message

began to come to mind just the way it had been described -
- one word, then two until, to my complete amazement and
gratefulness, I wrote the words that were imparted to me.

I knew as soon as the words began to form that the
message was incredibly significant because I immediately
recognized them from a very special and favorite bible
story - *The Book of Esther* - the Queen!

In addition to the story being about the beautiful
queen, this book held another precious meaning for me
personally. *The Book of Esther* is where I found my new
name written that had been mystically given to me many
years ago.

This is another significant spiritual event that I have
written about in more detail in my previous book.
However, briefly, my name *Anne Urne* was spoken to me
during a dreamlike meditative state when I heard the name
spelled out: "U-R-N-E." I wondered what this might
mean, and simply decided that it was *urn* spelled with a
silent *'e'* to match the spelling of my first name.

Then, while reading my bible one day I was taken
aback when in Chapter 3 of *Esther* I discovered my name!
I was reading *'the lot was cast into* **an urn***!'*

Oh, how many, many times I had read *The Book of Esther* after acquiring my new name and never noticed that it was written right there! The day I recognized those words as my name was so special. How can you describe such synchronicity such spiritual confirmation - such wonder in the way God works? You can't! His ways are overwhelming and indescribably awe inspiring!

Upon my return home from the seminar on Mary Magdalene I *knew* it was time to get my book out and do something with it. It was copyrighted, I had the ISBN number and all I had to do was get it printed and I could publish it. It had been so long since I had worked on the book, that I was now using a new computer and newer software. This technological transition presented even another marvelous surprise and synchronicity that confirmed it was time to publish this book.

When I opened the document that contained the cover for my book - I noticed some loopy symbols across the back cover page. I squinted to see what they were - and then copied one and enlarged it.

In my wildest imagination I couldn't have come up with anything that was more convincing than this that it was time to publish!

See for yourself what I found on the cover of my book:

♍

M for Mary, and a perfect Pisces fish that is symbolic for both Jesus and the goddess - together - in perfect union!

As I stared at the unexplained symbol on the back of my book, I recalled the seal that was given to Esther by the king to seal the letters that would save her people.

No wonder the tears were so hot and unstoppable when I was given the message that pierced my heart during that meditation on Mary Magdalene.

Those words, like my new name, are ingrained in my soul:

ASK

O QUEEN

FOR YOUR HALF

OF THE HEAVENLY KINGDOM

NOW!

This is the original cover Anne Urne used for the first printing. The vase represents her name - and the three roses are for Mother Mary, Mary Magdalene and St. Therese, the Little Flower.

TRUST ME

THE MYSTICAL STORY OF
MARY MAGDALENE

ANNE URNE

MORE ABOUT THE MYSTERIOUS SYMBOL

♍

While collaborating with Susan on the reprint of Trust Me, I asked her help in trying to recreate the symbol that had mysteriously appeared on my original manuscript. The old computer had crashed and the symbol would not translate on the new software.

Susan who had formerly studied astrology and knew all of the zodiac symbols was quick to inform me that my symbol was clearly the sign of Virgo! You can't imagine my surprise, delight and excitement. First, she had the symbol and could print it on future books. Then, the realization hit me. The impact of the Virgo symbol stamped on the story of the union of Mary Magdalene and Jesus lifted me to a higher joy!

The Virgin is the mother of Jesus - the original mother of Lulawa and Abel - and this symbol has it all!. "Virgo" symbol for the Virgin Mother, "M" for Maggie and the fish or Pisces symbol for Jesus. Lastly, I believe the Virgo symbol must represent the purity of the union and the presence of the Virgin Mother at that wedding in Cana.

Susan further enlightened me on the Virgo and Pisces symbols, telling me the sign Virgo is 180 degrees from Pisces making it the "other side" or opposite of Pisces so they are connected astrologically. There is no end to the synchronicities!

PREVIEW OF NEW BOOK
TO BE RELASED SOON

COMMUNION

The Communion of Saints

Anne Urne

FIRST EDITION

BOIS PUBLICATIONS
OKLAHOMA CITY, OKLAHOMA

October 6, 2009 – Oklahoma City - The Paris Plans
St. Therese and St. Mary Magdalene

I am so happy this morning. My cousin, Susan, decided to extend her stay in Paris another week so I can join her with my girl friend.

"Yes! I AM going to Paris!"

Today was another work day for me and as I drove to work I said my Novena to St. Therese. It is a daily prayer that I say on my drive to work downtown each morning and it includes five repetitions of the Our Father, Hail Mary and Glory Be to the Father. My prayers were full of thanksgiving and special thanks to all my French saints that I had called upon to help me get to Paris. I especially wanted to visit the country where my special patron saint, Therese, lived and the place where Mary Magdalene is believed to have been taken after the death of Jesus.

I never miss a morning visiting with St. Theresa and Maggie in my prayers. They are both very special to me.

I have a beautiful red haired doll that sits on a night stand near my bed. The doll came very unexpectedly as a gift from my aunt in California and coincidentally arrived right on my birthday a few years ago. I hadn't seen my aunt for decades and was totally surprised to get this beautiful gift from her. I called to thank her and she told me how she had been out with her husband and saw the doll. She said it reminded her of me as a little girl because of her beautiful long red curls.

My aunt was surprised and delighted to find out that her gift had arrived on my birthday, and I had more than one reason to celebrate this wonderful gift. At the time my doll arrived, I was right in the middle of writing the most exciting story ever about Mary Magdalene – another redhead. So, you guessed it, that doll's name is Maggie – my special name for Mary Magdalene.

Aunt Marilyn is the mother of my cousin, Susan that I am now planning to meet in Paris. We were very close as young children and visited often, had sleepovers, went to each other's birthday parties and were as close as sisters.

We were just young children growing up in Illinois when we were separated. I moved to Oklahoma with Mom and my sister, and later Susan moved to California with her mom and brother. Our moms were sisters and their Irish family in Illinois was a close knit bunch. That was back in the day when communication was nearly non-existent, compared to today's instant communications.

As the years went by there were occasional letters between our moms and maybe once a year that very expensive long distance phone call. So, this reunion with my cousin is a wonderful surprise and blessing after nearly forty years.

Today is a beautiful fall day, the sky is blue, the sun is shining brightly and the temperature is in the upper sixties. I finished saying my prayers as I neared downtown where I work. The commute takes about fifteen minutes when the traffic moves along smoothly and it is just the right amount of time to pray the novena.

When I arrived downtown I turned into the parking garage and circled up to the seventh floor and parked. I hummed a tune as I rode down the elevator to the ground floor and stepped out onto the sidewalk marveling at the gorgeous day that met me. My heart was full of thanksgiving and happiness over the news this morning that my cousin had emailed confirming plans for me to meet up with her in Paris.

I had just taken a few steps out of the garage when, out of nowhere, two girls approached me on the sidewalk. The first girl asked if they could speak to me just a moment, and quickly explained that they were not panhandlers. She told me they were stranded until the next day when Traveler's Aid would get them on a bus, but they were hungry and wondered if I could help them.

The young girl continued, saying, "My name is Maggie, and this is Theresa."

"Well," I answered her, "You definitely have my attention, because your names are those of my two favorite saints!"

At that moment, the girl named Theresa reached out, smiled and hugged me! I emptied my wallet! They smiled and thanked me.

Stunned, I proceeded down the sidewalk towards the office, and when I looked back they had disappeared.

What are the odds? Maggie and Theresa! I thought.

I knew beyond a doubt my new book, "Communion" was taking off – and I believed with all my heart that my special saints had manifested themselves to me.

And, I thought to myself, *"THERESA HUGGED ME!"*

This book is beginning to unfold around the saints. I am leaving in two weeks to visit Paris and London. My first trip abroad and I am so excited. The first thing I ordered was a book called *A Pilgrim's France*.

Later that week my book arrived and I took it to the bedroom to study about places to see in France. The moment I opened it and began flipping through the pages, I landed right on the picture and stories about St. Therese of Lisieux! This beautiful nun's picture was smiling up at me as I began reading about her and the places to visit. Of course I had read her book, *The Story of a Soul,* many times and it was one of my treasures, but it had been awhile since I had last looked at her book. So, now, I was enjoying reading about her again in my new book. When I reached the top of the second page while reclining on my bed, I bolted straight up as I read a quote from her book,

"*I will come down!*"

Her words brought me right back to that hug the other day, and I realized she had come down -- to me!

"Oh, St. Therese, what a treasure, adventure and blessing this book on the communions of saints is going to become. My anticipation of visiting your home is overwhelming."

Every day I pass the spot where I met Theresa and Maggie and smile. The spot is right in front of two glass doors to an apartment building. On each door the letter "M" is etched in the glass. Yes, on that very spot where I met the girls, the glass doors read: *M M.*

Oh, I love you Mary Magdalene!

I pray the Rosary often, being a Catholic girl, and those who are Catholic know that each decade has an assigned mystery that can be meditated upon while praying the Rosary. The official Catholic Mysteries are: Joyful, Luminous, Sorrowful and Glorious.

In honor of Mary Magdalene, I made up a personal set of mysteries to meditate upon in honor of Maggie when I pray the Rosary:

THE MARY MAGDALENE MYSTERIES

1. The Wedding at Cana;
2. Bathing the feet of Jesus with her tears and wiping them with her beautiful hair;
3. Anointing Jesus with fragrant nard from an urn;
4. Witnessing the Crucifixion of Jesus; and
5. The first to witness His Resurrection.